A HODDER CHRISTIAN BOOK OMNIBUS

HENRI J. M. NOUWEN

Life of the Beloved
Our Greatest Gift

LIFE OF THE BELOVED

Life of the Beloved

Spiritual Living in a Secular World

Henri J. M. Nouwen

Hodder & Stoughton

LONDON SYDNEY AUCKLAND

This Henri Nouwen Omnibus edition first published 2002 by Hodder and Stoughton,
a Division of Hodder Headline
0 340 78722 8

10 9 8 7 6 5 4 3 2 1

British Library Cataloguing in Publication Data
A record for this book is available at the British Library

Printed and bound in Great Britain by
The Guernsey Press Co. Ltd, Guernsey, C.I.

Hodder and Stoughton
A Division of Hodder Headline Ltd
338 Euston Road
London NW1 3BH

Life of the Beloved

First published in the United States by
The Crossroad Publishing Company
First published in Great Britain 1993
by Hodder and Stoughton
a division of Hodder Headline Limited

To Connie Ellis
in gratitude

Contents

Acknowledgments   7

Prologue: A Friendship Begins   9

BEING THE BELOVED   **23**

BECOMING THE BELOVED   **35**

     I.   TAKEN   43

     II.   BLESSED   55

     III.   BROKEN   69

     IV.   GIVEN   84

LIVING AS THE BELOVED   **101**

Epilogue: A Friendship Deepens   113

Acknowledgments

This book was written and made ready for publication with the support of many friends. I first of all want to thank Connie Ellis for her secretarial assistance and for the many ways in which she encouraged me to keep writing during busy times. I dedicate *Life of the Beloved* to her in deep gratitude for her faithful friendship and generous support. I am also grateful to Conrad Wieczorek for the many ways in which he offered his editorial assistance to Connie and myself in the final stages of the manuscript.

A special word of thanks goes to Patricia Beall, Diana Chambers, Gordon Cosby, Bart Gavigan, Steve Jenkinson, Sue Mosteller, Dolly Reisman, Susan Zimmerman, and my editor at Crossroad, Bob Heller, for their many encouraging words and concrete suggestions to bring this text to completion.

Finally I want to express my thanks to Peggy McDonnell, her family and friends, for their friendship and their generous financial support and to the Franciscan Community in Freiburg, Germany, who offered me a safe and prayerful place to write.

PROLOGUE

A Friendship Begins

This book is the fruit of a longstanding friendship, and you will read it with more profit, I believe, if I begin by telling you the story of this friendship. A little more than ten years ago, while I was teaching at Yale Divinity School, a young man arrived in my office to interview me for the Connecticut section of the Sunday edition of the *New York Times*. He introduced himself as Fred Bratman. As we sat down to talk, I quickly found myself taken hold of by a mixture of irritation and fascination. I was irritated because it was clear that this journalist was not terribly interested in doing what he was doing. Someone had suggested to him that I might be a good subject for a profile. He had followed up on the suggestion, but I couldn't detect any great eagerness to know me or any ardent desire to write about me. It was a journalist's job that had to be done, but could easily be done without. Nevertheless, there was also an element of fascination because I sensed, behind the mask of indifference, a spirit fully alive — eager to learn and to create. I somehow knew that I was face to face with a man full of great personal gifts, anxiously searching for a way to use them.

After a half-hour of questions that seemed of little interest to either of us, it became obvious that the interview had come to an end. An article would be written; a few people might read it, and there would be little, if any, outcome. The two of us knew this, and we both sensed that we could have put our time to better use.

Just as Fred was about to put his notebook back into his briefcase and say his customary "Thank you," I looked at him squarely and said, "Tell me, do you like your job?" Quite to my surprise, he replied, without much thought, "No, not really, but it's a job." Somewhat naively I responded, "If you don't like it, why do you do it? "For the money, of course," he said, and then, without further questioning from me, added, "Although I really love to write, doing these little newspaper profiles frustrates me because the limitations of length and form prevent me from doing justice to my subject. How, for example, can I say something in depth about you and your ideas when I can only use 750 words to express it? . . . but what choice do I have? . . . You have to make a living.

I should be happy to have at least this to do!" In his voice I heard both anger and resignation.

Suddenly it hit me that Fred was close to surrendering his dreams. He looked to me like a prisoner locked behind the bars of a society forcing him to work at something in which he didn't believe. Looking at him, I experienced a deep sympathy — more than that I dare say — a deep love for this man. Beneath the sarcasm and the cynicism I sensed a beautiful heart, a heart that wanted to give, to create, to live a fruitful life. His sharp mind, his openness about himself and the simple trust he put in me made me feel that our meeting could not just be something accidental. What was happening between us seemed to me quite similar to what happened when Jesus looked steadily at the rich young man and "was filled with love for him" (Mark 10:21).

Quite spontaneously I felt a strong desire rise up in me to liberate him from his imprisonment and to help him to discover how to fulfill his own deepest desires.

"What do you really want?" I asked.

"I want to write a novel, . . . but I'll never be able to do it."

"Is this something you really want?" I asked. He looked at me with surprise on his face and said with a smile, "Yes, it is, . . . but I'm also afraid because I've never written a novel, and maybe I don't have what it takes to be a novelist." "How will you find out?" I asked. "Well, I probably won't ever be able to find out. You need time, money and, most of all, talent, and I don't have any."

By now I had become angry at him, at society and, to some degree, at myself for letting things just be as they are. I felt a strong urge to break down all these walls of fear, convention, social expectations and self-deprecation, and I blurted out, "Why don't you quit your job and write your novel?" "I can't," he said.... I kept pushing him, "If you really want it, you can do it. You don't have to be the victim of time and money." At this point, I realized that I had become involved in a battle I was determined to win. He sensed my intensity and said, "Well, I'm just a simple journalist, and I guess I should be content with that." "No, you shouldn't," I said. "You should claim your deepest desire and do what you really want to do... time and money aren't the real issue." "What is?" he asked. "You are," I answered. "You have nothing to lose. You are young, full of energy, well trained.... Everything is possible for you.... Why let the world squeeze you in?... Why become a victim? You are free to do what you want — if, that is, you really want it!"

He looked at me with increasing surprise, wondering what it was that had gotten him into this bizarre conversation. "Well," he said, "I'd better go.... Maybe one day I will write my novel."

I stopped him, not wanting to let him off so easily. "Wait, Fred, I meant what I said. Follow your desire." With a touch of sarcasm in his voice, he said, "Sounds good to me!" I didn't want to let him go. I realized that my own convictions were at stake. I believe that people can make choices and make them according to their own best aspirations. I also believe that people seldom make these choices. Instead, they blame the world, the society and others for their "fate" and waste much of their life complaining. But I sensed, after our short verbal skirmish, that Fred was capable of jumping over his own fears and taking the risk of trusting himself. I knew also, however, that I had to jump first before he could, and so I said, "Fred, give up your job, come here for a year and write your novel. I will get the money somehow."

Later — many years later — Fred told me that, when I said this, he got very nervous and began questioning my motives. "What does this man really want of me?" he thought. "Why is he offering me money and time to write? I don't trust this. There must be something else going on here!" But, instead of saying any of this, he only objected, "I am a Jew, and this is a Christian seminary." I pushed his objection aside. "We will make you a scholar in residence....You can do what you like....People here will love having a novelist in the house, and, meanwhile, you can learn something about Christianity and Judaism too."

A few months later, Fred came to Yale Divinity School and spent a year there trying to write his novel. It was never written, but we became close friends, and today, many years later, I am writing this book as a fruit of that friendship.

During the ten years or more that followed our time together at Yale, both Fred and I lived lives very different from what we anticipated when we first met. Fred lived through a very painful divorce; remarried; and now he and his wife, Robin, are expecting their first child. Meanwhile, he worked at different jobs, not very satisfying at first, until he found a position that offered him ample scope for the exercise of his creative abilities. My own journey was no more predictable. I left the academic world, went to Latin America, tried the academic world again and finally settled in a community with people who have a mental handicap and their assistants. There was much struggle, much pain and much joy in both our lives, and we were able to share these experiences at length during regular visits. As time passed, we grew closer and became more and more aware of the importance of our friendship for each other, even though busyness, distance and personal lifestyles often stood in the way of our seeing each other as much as we wanted.

From the very beginning of our friendship, we were quite conscious of our radically different religious backgrounds. At first, it seemed as if this would make it hard to support each other spiritually. Fred respected me as a Catholic priest and showed sincere interest in my life and work, but Christianity in general and the Catholic Church in particular were little more than one of his many objects of interest. For myself, I could quite easily understand Fred's secular Judaism, despite my feeling that he would gain much by growing closer to his own spiritual heritage. I vividly remember once telling Fred that it would be good for him to read the Hebrew Bible. He protested, "It doesn't speak to me. It is a strange faraway world...." "Well," I said, "read at least the Book of Qoheleth [Ecclesiastes], the one that opens with the words: 'Vanity of vanities.... All is vanity.'"

The next day Fred said, "I read it.... I never realized that there was a place for a skeptic in the Bible...one of my type.... That's very reassuring!" I remember thinking, "There is much more than a skeptic in you."

As we both grew older and became a little less concerned about success, career, fame, money and time, questions of meaning and purpose came more into the center of our relationship.

In the midst of the many changes in our lives, both of us came into closer touch with our deeper desires. Different though our circumstances were, we both had to deal with the pains of rejection and separation, and both of us realized increasingly our desire for intimacy and friendship. To avoid being drowned in bitterness and resentment, we both had to draw on our deepest spiritual resources. Differences became less important, similarities more obvious. As our friendship grew deeper and stronger, our desire for a common spiritual foundation became more explicit.

One day, while walking on Columbus Avenue in New York City, Fred turned to me and said, "Why don't you write something about the spiritual life for me and my friends?" Fred was familiar with most of what I had written. Often he had given solid advice on form and style, but seldom did he feel connected with the content. As a Jew, living in the secular world of New York City, he couldn't find much comfort or support in words that were so explicitly Christian and so clearly based on a long life in the Church. "It is good stuff," he often said, "but not for me." He felt strongly that his own experience and that of his friends required another tone, another language, another spiritual wavelength.

As I gradually came to know Fred's friends and got a feel for their interests and concerns, I better understood Fred's remarks about the need for a spirituality that speaks to men and women in a secularized society. Much of my thinking and writing presupposed a familiarity with concepts and images that for many centuries had nourished the spiritual life of Christians and Jews, but for many people these concepts and images had lost their power to bring them into touch with their spiritual center.

Fred's idea that I say something about the spirit that his friends and he "could hear" stayed with me. He was asking me to respond to the great spiritual hunger and thirst that exist in countless people who walk the streets of big cities. He was calling me to speak a word of hope to people who no longer came to churches or synagogues and for whom priests and rabbis were no longer the obvious counselors.

"You have something to say," Fred kept telling me, "but you keep saying it to people who least need to hear it.... What about us young, ambitious, secular men and women wondering what life is all about after all? Can you speak to us with the same conviction as you speak to those who share your tradition, your language and your vision?"

Fred was not the only one to ask me such questions. What Fred had expressed so clearly was coming at me from many other directions as well. I heard it from people in my community who had no religious background and for whom the Bible was a strange, confusing book. I heard it from members of my family who had long ago left the Church and had no desire ever to return. I heard it from lawyers, doctors and businessmen whose lives had taken up all their energy and for whom Saturday and Sunday were little more than a brief respite to gain enough strength to re-enter the arena on Monday morning. I heard it, too, from young men and women beginning to feel the many demands of a society that claimed their attention, but fearing at the same time that it was not going to offer them much in the way of real life.

Fred's question became much more than the intriguing suggestion of a young New York intellectual. It became the plea that arose on all sides — wherever I was open to hear it. And, in the end, it became for me the most pertinent and the most urgent of all demands: "Speak to us about the deepest yearning of our hearts, about our many wishes, about hope; not about the many strategies for survival, but about trust; not about new methods of satisfying our emotional needs, but about love. Speak to us about a vision larger than our changing perspectives and about a voice deeper than the clamorings of our mass media. Yes, speak to us about something or someone greater than ourselves. Speak to us about...God."

"Who am I to speak about such things?" I answered. "My own life is too small for that. I don't have the experience, the knowledge or the language you are asking for. You and your friends live in a world so different from my own."

Fred didn't give me much room. "You can do it. ...You have to do it....If you don't, who will?... Visit me more often; talk to my friends; look attentively at what you see, and listen carefully to what you hear. You will discover a cry welling up from the depths of the human heart that has remained unheard because there was no one to listen."

Fred's words made me think of his apartment on 75th Street: a cozy place surrounded by a harsh world. When Fred first brought me there, many years ago, he drew my attention to the bareness of the building's entrance hall. "Everything is stolen," he said. "The chandelier, the marble on the walls, whatever has any value is ripped off and taken, often in broad daylight." As the elevator took us to the eleventh floor, I felt an eerie silence among the passengers who were almost elbow to elbow. How close and yet how far apart. Fred needed two keys to open his apartment door, and he had to close tightly the double windows protected by iron bars to keep the noise of Columbus Avenue from invading every corner of his space. Yes, a pleasant home, but, when we finally found our way to it, a whole story of violence and oppression, fear and suspicion, anguish and agony, had already been told. There I learned about Fred's daily doings: leaving his apartment in the early morning and vanishing into the crowds on his way to work; reading the morning paper on the subway and working on a financial newsletter in a little office cubicle; taking his lunch with a colleague in a noisy restaurant, and spending the afternoon with countless phone calls and faxes, and then vanishing once again into the crowds, finding his way back to his cozy haven.

What could I possibly say to a man living in this kind of place with this kind of rhythm? What could I possibly say to a world of rushing taxicabs, glass-covered office towers and show business going on day and night? And still, wasn't I prepared during the many years of study, prayer and encounters to be able to speak words of hope to precisely this world?

"But how? How?" I said to Fred, while feeling resistance and my eagerness to respond locked in an inner battle. His answer: "Speak from that place in your heart where you are most yourself. Speak directly, simply, lovingly, gently and without any apologies. Tell us what you see and want us to see; tell us what you hear and want us to hear.... Trust your own heart. The words will come. There is nothing to fear. Those who need you most will help you most. You can be sure that I will."

And now, as I begin at last to write, I know that I can do so only when I stay very close to Fred and his friends. They called me to be who I want to be, but they gave me, as well, the assurance of their love.

I have chosen to speak directly — as I would in a personal letter. By keeping Fred and his friends at the center of my attention, I can best express what is in my heart. I am not able to deal with all the burning issues of our time and society, but I am able to write to a dear friend whom I came to know and love as a fellow-traveler searching for life, light and truth. I hope that through my being so personal and direct many may want to "listen in" and even join in this spiritual search.

BEING
the BELOVED

EVER SINCE YOU ASKED ME to write for you and your friends about the spiritual life, I have been wondering if there might be one word I would most want you to remember when you finished reading all I wish to say. Over the past year, that special word has gradually emerged from the depths of my own heart. It is the word "Beloved," and I am convinced that it has been given to me for the sake of you and your friends. Being a Christian, I first learned this word from the story of the baptism of Jesus of Nazareth. "No sooner had Jesus come up out of the water than he saw the heavens torn apart and the Spirit, like a dove, descending on him. And a voice came from heaven: 'You are my Son, the Beloved;

my favor rests on you.'" For many years I had read these words and even reflected upon them in sermons and lectures, but it is only since our talks in New York that they have taken on a meaning far beyond the boundaries of my own tradition. Our many conversations led me to the inner conviction that the words, "You are my Beloved" revealed the most intimate truth about all human beings, whether they belong to any particular tradition or not.

Fred, all I want to say to you is "You are the Beloved," and all I hope is that you can hear these words as spoken to you with all the tenderness and force that love can hold. My only desire is to make these words reverberate in every corner of your being — "You are the Beloved."

The greatest gift my friendship can give to you is the gift of your Belovedness. I can give that gift only insofar as I have claimed it for myself. Isn't that what friendship is all about: giving to each other the gift of our Belovedness?

Yes, there is that voice, the voice that speaks from above and from within and that whispers softly or declares loudly: "You are my Beloved, on you my favor rests." It certainly is not easy to hear that voice in a world filled with voices that shout: "You are no good, you are ugly; you are worthless; you are despicable, you are nobody — unless you can demonstrate the opposite."

These negative voices are so loud and so persistent that it is easy to believe them. That's the great trap. It is the trap of self-rejection. Over the years, I have come to realize that the greatest trap in our life is not success, popularity or power, but self-rejection. Success, popularity and power can, indeed, present a great temptation, but their seductive quality often comes from the way they are part of the much larger temptation to self-rejection. When we have come to believe in the voices that call us worthless and unlovable, then success, popularity and power are easily perceived as attractive solutions. The real trap, however, is self-rejection. I am constantly surprised at how quickly I give in to this temptation. As soon as someone accuses me or criticizes me, as soon as I am rejected, left alone or abandoned, I find myself thinking: "Well, that proves once again that I am a nobody." Instead of taking a critical look at the circumstances or trying to understand my own and others' limitations, I tend to blame myself — not just for what I did, but for who I am. My dark side says: "I am no good.... I deserve to be pushed aside, forgotten, rejected and abandoned."

Maybe you think that you are more tempted by arrogance than by self-rejection. But isn't arrogance, in fact, the other side of self-rejection? Isn't arrogance putting yourself on a pedestal to avoid being seen as you see yourself? Isn't arrogance, in the final analysis, just another way of dealing with the feelings of worthlessness? Both self-rejection and arrogance pull us out of the common reality of existence and make a gentle community of people extremely difficult, if not impossible, to attain. I know too well that beneath my arrogance there lies much self-doubt, just as there is a great amount of pride hidden in my self-rejection. Whether I am inflated or deflated, I lose touch with my truth and distort my vision of reality.

I hope you can somehow identify in yourself the temptation to self-rejection, whether it manifests itself in arrogance or in low self-esteem. Not seldom, self-rejection is simply seen as the neurotic expression of an insecure person. But neurosis is often the psychic manifestation of a much deeper human darkness: the darkness of not feeling truly welcome in human existence. Self-rejection is the greatest enemy of the spiritual life because it contradicts the sacred voice that calls us the "Beloved." Being the Beloved expresses the core truth of our existence.

I am putting this so directly and so simply because, though the experience of being the Beloved has never been completely absent from my life, I never claimed it as my core truth. I kept running around it in large or small circles, always looking for someone or something able to convince me of my Belovedness. It was as if I kept refusing to hear the voice that speaks from the very depth of my being and says: "You are my Beloved, on you my favor rests." That voice has always been there, but it seems that I was much more eager to listen to other, louder voices saying: "Prove that you are worth something; do something relevant, spectacular or powerful, and then you will earn the love you so desire." Meanwhile, the soft, gentle voice that speaks in the silence and solitude of my heart remained unheard or, at least, unconvincing.

That soft, gentle voice that calls me the Beloved has come to me in countless ways. My parents, friends, teachers, students and the many strangers who crossed my path have all sounded that voice in different tones. I have been cared for by many people with much tenderness and gentleness. I have been taught and instructed with much patience and perseverance. I have been encouraged to keep going when I was ready to give up and was stimulated to try again when I failed. I have been rewarded and praised for success...but, somehow, all of these signs of love were not sufficient to convince me that I was the Beloved. Beneath all my seemingly strong self-confidence there remained the question: "If all those who shower me with so much attention could see me and know me in my innermost self, would they still love me?" That agonizing question, rooted in my inner shadow, kept persecuting me and made me run away from the very place where that quiet voice calling me the Beloved could be heard.

I think you understand what I am talking about.

Aren't you, like me, hoping that some person, thing or event will come along to give you that final feeling of inner well-being you desire? Don't you often hope: "May this book, idea, course, trip, job, country or relationship fulfill my deepest desire." But as long as you are waiting for that mysterious moment you will go on running helter-skelter, always anxious and restless, always lustful and angry, never fully satisfied. You know that this is the compulsiveness that keeps us going and busy, but at the same time makes us wonder whether we are getting anywhere in the long run. This is the way to spiritual exhaustion and burn-out. This is the way to spiritual death.

Well, you and I don't have to kill ourselves. We are the Beloved. We are intimately loved long before our parents, teachers, spouses, children and friends loved or wounded us. That's the truth of our lives. That's the truth I want you to claim for yourself. That's the truth spoken by the voice that says, "You are my Beloved."

Listening to that voice with great inner attentiveness, I hear at my center words that say: "I have called you by name, from the very beginning. You are mine and I am yours. You are my Beloved, on you my favor rests. I have molded you in the depths of the earth and knitted you together in your mother's womb. I have carved you in the palms of my hands and hidden you in the shadow of my embrace. I look at you with infinite tenderness and care for you with a care more intimate than that of a mother for her child. I have counted every hair on your head and guided you at every step. Wherever you go, I go with you, and wherever you rest, I keep watch. I will give you food that will satisfy all your hunger and drink that will quench all your thirst. I will not hide my face from you. You know me as your own as I know you as my own. You belong to me. I am your father, your mother, your brother, your sister, your lover and your spouse ... yes, even your child ... wherever you are I will be. Nothing will ever separate us. We are one."

Every time you listen with great attentiveness to the voice that calls you the Beloved, you will discover within yourself a desire to hear that voice longer and more deeply. It is like discovering a well in the desert. Once you have touched wet ground, you want to dig deeper.

I have been doing a lot of digging lately and I know that I am just beginning to see a little stream bubbling up through the dry sand. I have to keep digging because that little stream comes from a huge reservoir beneath the desert of my life. The word "digging" might not be the best word, since it suggests hard and painful work that finally leads me to the place where I can quench my thirst. Perhaps all we need to do is remove the dry sand that covers the well. There may be quite a pile of dry sand in our lives, but the One who so desires to quench our thirst will help us to remove it. All we really need is a great desire to find the water and drink from it.

You have lived fewer years than I. You may still want to look around a little more and a little longer so as to become convinced that the spiritual life is worth all your energy. But I do feel a certain impatience toward you because I don't want you to waste too much of your time! I have fewer years ahead of me than behind me. For you, I hope the opposite is true. Therefore, I want to assure you already, now, that you do not have to get caught in searches that lead only to entanglement. Neither do you have to become the victim of a manipulative world or get trapped in any kind of addiction. You can choose to reach out now to true inner freedom and find it ever more fully.

So, if you are interested in starting on the journey of the Beloved, I have a lot more to say to you, because the journey of the spiritual life calls not only for determination, but also for a certain knowledge of the terrain to be crossed. I don't want you to have to wander about in the desert for forty years as did our spiritual forebears. I don't even want you to dwell there as long as I did. You are very dear to me, a friend whom I truly love. Although it remains true that everyone has to learn for him- or herself, I still believe that we can prevent those we love from making the same mistakes we did. In the terrain of the spiritual life, we need guides. In the pages that I now want to write for you, I would like to be your guide. I hope you are still interested in walking along.

BECOMING
the BELOVED

Enfleshing the Truth

DEAR FRIEND, being the Beloved is the origin and the fulfillment of the life of the Spirit. I say this because, as soon as we catch a glimpse of this truth, we are put on a journey in search of the fullness of that truth and we will not rest until we can rest in that truth. From the moment we claim the truth of being the Beloved, we are faced with the call to become who we are. Becoming the Beloved is the great spiritual journey we have to make. Augustine's words: "My soul is restless until it rests in you, O God," capture well this journey. I know that the fact that I am always searching for God, always struggling to discover the fullness of Love, always yearning for the complete truth, tells me that I have already been given a taste of God, of Love and of Truth. I can only look for something that I have, to some degree, already found. How can I search for beauty and truth unless that beauty and truth are already known to me in the depth of my heart? It seems that all of us human beings have deep inner memories of the paradise that we have lost. Maybe the word "innocence" is better than the word "paradise." We were innocent before we started feeling guilty; we were in the light before we entered into the darkness; we were at home before we started to search for a home. Deep in the recesses of our minds and hearts there lies hidden the treasure we seek. We know its preciousness, and we know that it holds the gift we most desire: a life stronger than death.

If it is true that we not only are the Beloved, but also have to *become* the Beloved; if it is true that we not only *are* children of God, but also have to *become* children of God; if it is true that we not only *are* brothers and sisters, but also have to *become* brothers and sisters...if all that is true, how then can we get a grip on this process of becoming? If the spiritual life is not simply a way of being, but also a way of becoming, what then is the nature of this becoming?

You are enough of a pragmatist to ask how we get from the first to the second innocence, from the first to the second childhood, from being the Beloved to fully becoming it. This is such an important question because it forces us to let go of any romanticism or idealism and to deal with the utter concreteness of our daily lives. *Becoming the Beloved means letting the truth of our Belovedness become enfleshed in everything we think, say or do.* It entails a long and painful process of appropriation or, better, incarnation. As long as "being the Beloved" is little more than a beautiful thought or a lofty idea that hangs above my life to keep me from becoming depressed, nothing really changes. What is required is to become the Beloved in the commonplaces of my daily existence and, bit by bit, to close the gap that exists between what I know myself to be and the countless specific realities of everyday life. Becoming the Beloved is pulling the truth revealed to me from above down into the ordinariness of what I am, in fact, thinking of, talking about and doing from hour to hour.

When I think about your life and the lives of Robin and your friends, I am quite aware of the pressures you undergo. You and Robin live in the middle of New York in a small apartment; you have to keep working to earn enough for your rent and your food; you have thousands of little things to do, from making phone calls to writing letters, buying and cooking food, staying in touch with family and friends and remaining informed about what happens in your city, your country and your world. All of that seems quite a lot for one person, and it is usually these very simple concrete things of daily living that provide the raw materials for our conversations. The question, "How are you doing?" usually leads to very down-to-earth stories about marriage, family, health, work, money, friends and plans for the immediate future. It seldom, however, leads to deep thoughts about the origin and goal of our existence. Still, I am thoroughly convinced that the origin and goal of our existence have everything to do with the ways we think, talk and act in our daily lives. When our deepest truth is that we are the Beloved and when our greatest joy and peace come from fully claiming that truth, it follows that this has to become visible and tangible in the ways we eat and drink, talk and love, play and work. When the deepest currents of our life no longer have any influence on the waves at the surface, then our vitality will eventually ebb, and we will end up listless and bored even when we are busy.

So, my task now is to write about that process of becoming the Beloved as it can be pinpointed in our very concrete daily lives. What I will attempt to describe are the movements of the Spirit as they take place within us and around us. As you know, we live in a very "psychological" age. We know a lot about our emotions, passions and feelings. We are quite aware of the many connections between our early experiences and our present behaviors. We have become quite sophisticated about our own psychosexual development and can easily identify our moments of victimization and our moments of real freedom. We know about being defensive; we know about projecting our own needs and fears onto others, and we know that our self-doubts can easily get in the way of our creativity. My question is whether it is possible to be as articulate about our spiritual journey as we are about our psychological journey. Can we come into touch with that mysterious process of becoming the Beloved in the same specific way as we can come into touch with the "dynamics" of our psyches?

You may wonder if psychodynamics are really so different from the movements of the Spirit. I think they are, even though they connect and intersect in many ways. What I want to describe is how the movements of the Spirit of love manifest themselves in our daily struggles and how we can develop disciplines to identify these movements and respond to them in our actions.

To identify the movements of the Spirit in our lives, I have found it helpful to use four words: taken, blessed, broken and given. These words summarize my life as a priest because each day, when I come together around the table with members of my community, I take bread, bless it, break it and give it. These words also summarize my life as a Christian because, as a Christian, I am called to become bread for the world: bread that is taken, blessed, broken and given. Most importantly, however, they summarize my life as a human being because in every moment of my life somewhere, somehow the taking, the blessing, the breaking and the giving are happening.

I must tell you at this point that these four words have become the most important words of my life. Only gradually has their meaning become known to me, and I feel that I won't ever know their full profundity. They are the most personal as well as the most universal words. They express the most spiritual as well as the most secular truth. They speak about the most divine as well as the most human behavior. They reach high as well as low, embrace God as well as all people. They succinctly express the complexity of life and embrace its ever-unfolding mystery. They are the keys to understanding not only the lives of the great prophets of Israel and the life of Jesus of Nazareth, but also our own lives. I have chosen them not only because they are so deeply engraved in my being, but also because, through them, I have come into touch with the ways of becoming the Beloved of God.

I

TAKEN

To become the Beloved we, first of all, have to claim that we are taken. That might sound very strange at first, and, still, to be taken is essential in becoming the Beloved. As I have mentioned already, we can desire to become the Beloved only when we know that we already are the Beloved. Therefore, the first step in the spiritual life is to acknowledge with our whole being that we already have been taken.

It might help at this point if, instead of "take," which is a somewhat cold and brittle word, we used a warmer, softer word with the same meaning: the word "choose." As children of God, we are God's chosen ones.

I hope that the word "chosen" speaks to you. It must be for you a word with very special connotations. As a Jew, you know the positive and the negative associations in being considered one of God's chosen people. You often told me about the rich heritage of your family, the deep faith of your grandparents and the many traditions that connected your parents with the sacred history of your people. But you also told me about the cruel pogroms in the "old" country and the long and painful journey that brought your mother and father to America. Although you yourself have not suffered directly from persecution, you are quite aware of how much it is part of your story and how frighteningly close it is to the surface of your life. You showed me that anti-Semitism is always lurking around in one form or another, and recent events, both in Europe and in the United States, only confirm your conviction that "blaming the Jews" is not something of the past. I wouldn't be surprised if a part of you protests against the idea of being chosen. I recognize this in my own life. Being an ordained priest, I was often treated as a special person, as "set aside," as chosen to be different. Often I have tried to show or to prove that I was "just me" (one way to explain the "J. M." in my name!) and that I had no desire to be put on a pedestal and treated as a special person. I sensed, as you obviously do, that when you are treated as the chosen one, you are as liable to be persecuted as admired.

Still, I do believe deeply that, in order to live a spiritual life, we have to claim for ourselves that we are "taken" or "chosen." Let me try to expand a bit on these words. When I know that I am chosen, I know that I have been seen as a special person. Someone has noticed me in my uniqueness and has expressed a desire to know me, to come closer to me, to love me. When I write to you that, as the Beloved, we are God's chosen ones, I mean that we have been seen by God from all eternity and seen as unique, special, precious beings. It is very hard for me to express well the depth of meaning the word "chosen" has for me, but I hope you are willing to listen to me from within. From all eternity, long before you were born and became a part of history, you existed in God's heart. Long before your parents admired you or your friends acknowledged your gifts or your teachers, colleagues and employers encouraged you, you were already "chosen." The eyes of love had seen you as precious, as of infinite beauty, as of eternal value. When love chooses, it chooses with a perfect sensitivity for the unique beauty of the chosen one, and it chooses without making anyone else feel excluded.

We touch here a great spiritual mystery: to be chosen does not mean that others are rejected. It is very hard to conceive of this in a competitive world such as ours. All my memories of being chosen are linked to memories of others not being chosen. When I was not chosen for a soccer team, not chosen to be the leader of the Boy Scout patrol, or when I was chosen to be the "senior" of my ordination class, or to be honored with special awards, there were always tears alongside smiles and smiles alongside tears. Competition and comparison were always there. How often I needed the words: "The fact that you are not chosen does not mean that you are not good, only that someone else is a little better." But even these words were seldom consoling because the feeling of rejection was always there. And when I was chosen and selected as the best, I was always aware of how disappointed others were at not being in my place. It was then that I needed to hear the words: "The fact that you are chosen does not mean that others are not good, only that you are a little better." But, again, these words did not help very much because I was unable to make the others feel as happy as I. In this world, to be chosen simply means to be set apart in contrast to others. You know how in our extremely competitive society the "chosen ones" are looked at with special attention. Whole magazines are dedicated to "heroes" of sport, film, music, acting and other ways of excelling. They are the "chosen ones" and their devotees, whether readers, listeners or viewers, try to extract some vicarious pleasure from knowing them or being close to them.

To be chosen as the Beloved of God is something radically different. Instead of excluding others, it includes others. Instead of rejecting others as less valuable, it accepts others in their own uniqueness.

It is not a competitive, but a compassionate choice. Our minds have great difficulty in coming to grips with such a reality. Maybe our minds will never understand it. Perhaps it is only our hearts that can accomplish this. Every time we hear about "chosen people," "chosen talents" or "chosen friends," we almost automatically start thinking about elites and find ourselves not far from feelings of jealousy, anger or resentment. Not seldom has the perception of others as being chosen led to aggression, violence and war.

But I beg you, do not surrender the word "chosen" to the world. Dare to claim it as your own, even when it is constantly misunderstood. You must hold on to the truth that you are the chosen one. That truth is the bedrock on which you can build a life as the Beloved. When you lose touch with your chosenness, you expose yourself to the temptation of self-rejection, and that temptation undermines the possibility of ever growing as the Beloved.

As I look within as well as around myself, I am overwhelmed by the dark voices telling me, "You are nothing special; you are just another person among millions; your life is just one more mouth to feed, your needs just one more problem to solve." These voices are increasingly powerful, especially in a time marked by so many broken relationships. Many children never feel really welcomed in the world. Beneath their nervous smiles, there is often the question: "Am I really wanted?" Some young people even hear their mothers say: "I hadn't really expected you, but once I found out I was pregnant I decided to have you anyway.... You were sort of an accident." Words or attitudes such as these do nothing to make a person feel "chosen." Our world is full of people who question whether it would have been better had they not been born. When we do not feel loved by those who gave us life, we often suffer our whole life long from a low self-esteem that can lead easily to depression, despair and even suicide.

In the midst of this extremely painful reality, we have to dare to reclaim the truth that we are God's chosen ones, even when our world does not choose us. As long as we allow our parents, siblings, teachers, friends and lovers to determine whether we are chosen or not, we are caught in the net of a suffocating world that accepts or rejects us according to its own agenda of effectivity and control. Often this reclaiming is an arduous task, a lifelong work because the world persists in its efforts to pull us into the darkness of self-doubt, low self-esteem, self-rejection and depression. And this because it is as insecure, fearful, self-deprecating people that we can most easily be used and manipulated by the powers surrounding us. The great spiritual battle begins — and never ends — with the reclaiming of our chosenness. Long before any human being saw us, we are seen by God's loving eyes. Long before anyone heard us cry or laugh, we are heard by our God who is all ears for us. Long before any person spoke to us in this world, we are spoken to by the voice of eternal love. Our preciousness, uniqueness and individuality are not given to us by those who meet us in clock-time — our brief chronological existence — but by the One who has chosen us with an everlasting love, a love that existed from all eternity and will last through all eternity.

How do we get in touch with our chosenness when we are surrounded by rejections? I have already said that this involves a real spiritual struggle. Are there any guidelines in this struggle? Let me try to formulate a few.

First of all, you have to keep unmasking the world about you for what it is: manipulative, controlling, power-hungry and, in the long run, destructive. The world tells you many lies about who you are, and you simply have to be realistic enough to remind yourself of this. Every time you feel hurt, offended or rejected, you have to dare to say to yourself: "These feelings, strong as they may be, are not telling me the truth about myself. The truth, even though I cannot feel it right now, is that I am the chosen child of God, precious in God's eyes, called the Beloved from all eternity and held safe in an everlasting embrace."

Secondly, you have to keep looking for people and places where your truth is spoken and where you are reminded of your deepest identity as the chosen one. Yes, we must dare to opt consciously for our chosenness and not allow our emotions, feelings or passions to seduce us into self-rejection. The synagogues, the churches, the many communities of faith, the different support groups helping us with our addictions, family, friends, teachers and students: all of these can become reminders of our truth. The limited, sometimes broken, love of those who share our humanity can often point us to the truth of who we are: precious in God's eyes. This truth is not simply an inner truth that emerges from our center. It is also a truth that is revealed to us by the One who has chosen us. That is why we have to keep listening to the many men and women in history who, through their lives and their words, call us back to it.

Thirdly, you have to celebrate your chosenness constantly. This means saying "thank you" to God for having chosen you, and "thank you" to all who remind you of your chosenness. Gratitude is the most fruitful way of deepening your consciousness that you are not an "accident," but a divine choice. It is important to realize how often we have had chances to be grateful and have not used them. When someone is kind to us, when an event turns out well, when a problem is solved, a relationship restored, a wound healed, there are very concrete reasons to offer thanks: be it with words, with flowers, with a

letter, a card, a phone call or just a gesture of affection. However, precisely the same situations also
offer us occasions to be critical, skeptical, even cyn-
ical because, when someone is kind to us, we can
question his or her motives; when an event turns out
well, it could always have turned out better; when
a problem is solved, there often emerges another
in its place; when a relationship is restored, there
is always the question: "For how long?"; when a
wound is healed, there still can be some leftover
pain....Where there is reason for gratitude, there
can always be found a reason for bitterness. It is
here that we are faced with the freedom to make a
decision. We can decide to be grateful or to be bitter.
We can decide to recognize our chosenness in the
moment or we can decide to focus on the shadow
side. When we persist in looking at the shadow side,
we will eventually end up in the dark. I see this
every day in our community. The core members,
the men and women with mental disabilities, have
many reasons to be bitter. Many of them experience
deep loneliness, rejection from family members or
friends, the unfulfilled desire to have a partner in
life, and the constant frustration of always needing assistance. Still, they choose mostly not to be
bitter, but grateful for the many small gifts of their
lives — for an invitation to dinner, for a few days of
retreat or a birthday celebration and, most of all, for
their daily life in community with people who offer

friendship and support. They choose gratitude over bitterness and they become a great source of hope and inspiration for all their assistants who, although not mentally disabled, also have to make that same choice. When we keep claiming the light, we will find ourselves becoming more and more radiant. What fascinates me so much is that every time we decide to be grateful it will be easier to see new things to be grateful for. Gratitude begets gratitude, just as love begets love.

I hope that these three guidelines for getting in touch with your chosenness can help you in your daily life. For me, they are the spiritual disciplines for my life as the chosen one. It is not easy to practice them, especially during times of crisis. Before I know it, I find myself complaining again, brooding again about some rejection and plotting ways to take revenge, but, when I keep my disciplines close to my heart, I am able to step over my shadow into the light of my truth.

Before concluding these thoughts about "being chosen," I want to impress upon you the importance of this truth for our relationships with others. When we claim and constantly reclaim the truth of being the chosen ones, we soon discover within ourselves a deep desire to reveal to others their own chosenness. Instead of making us feel that we are better, more precious or valuable than others, our awareness of being chosen opens our eyes to the chosenness of others. That is the great joy of being chosen: the discovery that others are chosen as well. In the house of God there are many mansions. There is a place for everyone — a unique, special place. Once we deeply trust that we ourselves are precious in God's eyes, we are able to recognize the preciousness of others and their unique places in God's heart. This makes me think of Helen, one of the handicapped members of our community. When she came to Daybreak a few years ago, I felt quite distant from her, even a bit afraid. She lived in a little world of her own, only uttering distracting noises and never making any personal contact. But as we came to know her better and trusted that she, too, has a unique gift to offer, she gradually came out of her isolation, started to smile at us and became a great source of joy for the whole community.

I now realize that I had to be in touch with my own goodness to discover the unique goodness of Helen. As long as my self-doubts and fears guided me, I couldn't create the space for Helen to reveal to me her beauty. But once I claimed my own chosenness, I could be with Helen as a person who had much, very much, to offer me. It is impossible to compete for God's love. God's love is a love that includes all people — each one in his or her uniqueness. It is only when we have claimed our own place in God's love that we can experience this all-embracing, non-comparing love and feel safe, not only with God, but also with all our brothers and sisters.

You and I know how true-to-life this all is. We have been friends now for many years. In the beginning there was some comparing, some jealousy, some competition. But as we grew older and became more sure in our own uniqueness, most, if not all, of this rivalry vanished, and we were more able to affirm and call forth each other's gifts. I feel so good being with you because I know that you enjoy me for who I am and not just for what I can do for you. And you feel good when I come to visit you because you know that I marvel in your kindness, your goodness and your many gifts — not because they prove helpful for me, but simply because of you. Deep friendship is a calling forth of each other's chosenness and a mutual affirmation of being precious in God's eyes. Your life and my life are, each of them, one-of-a-kind. No one has lived your life or my life before, and no one will ever live them again. Our lives are unique stones in the mosaic of human existence — priceless and irreplaceable.

Being chosen is the basis for being the Beloved. It is a lifelong struggle to claim that chosenness, but also a lifelong joy. The more fully we claim it, the more easily will we also discover another aspect of being the Beloved: our blessedness. Let me speak to you about that now.

II

BLESSED

As the Beloved children of God, we are blessed. The word "blessing" has become very important for me over the past few years, and you are one of the friends who made it important for me.

Do you remember how one Saturday morning in New York City you took me to the synagogue? When we arrived, we discovered that there was to be a bar mitzvah. A young man, thirteen years old, was declared adult by his congregation. For the first time, he gave leadership to the service. He read from the Book of Genesis and gave a short sermon about the importance of caring for our environment. He was affirmed by the rabbi and his friends and blessed by his parents. It was the first time that I had witnessed a bar mitzvah, and I was deeply moved — most of all by the parents' blessing. I still hear the father saying: "Son, whatever will happen to you in your life, whether you will have success or not, become important or not, will be healthy or not, always remember how much your mother and I love you." When he said this in front of the congregation, looking gently at the boy standing before him, tears came to my eyes, and I thought: "What a grace such a blessing is."

I am increasingly aware of how much we fearful, anxious, insecure human beings are in need of a blessing. Children need to be blessed by their parents and parents by their children. We all need each other's blessings — masters and disciples, rabbis and students, bishops and priests, doctors and patients.

Let me first tell you what I mean by the word "blessing." In Latin, to bless is *benedicere*. The word "benediction" that is used in many churches means literally: speaking (*dictio*) well (*bene*) or saying good things of someone. That speaks to me. I need to hear good things said of me, and I know how much you have the same need. Nowadays, we often say: "We have to affirm each other." Without affirmation, it is hard to live well. To give someone a blessing is the most significant affirmation we can offer. It is more than a word of praise or appreciation; it is more than pointing out someone's talents or good deeds; it is more than putting someone in the light. To give a blessing is to affirm, to say "yes" to a person's Belovedness. And more than that: to give a blessing creates the reality of which it speaks. There is a lot of mutual admiration in this world, just as there is a lot of mutual condemnation. A blessing goes beyond the distinction between admiration or condemnation, between virtues or vices, between good deeds or evil deeds. A blessing touches the original goodness of the other and calls forth his or her Belovedness.

Not long ago, in my own community, I had a very personal experience of the power of a real blessing. Shortly before I started a prayer service in one of our houses, Janet, a handicapped member of our community, said to me: "Henri, can you give me a blessing?" I responded in a somewhat automatic way by tracing with my thumb the sign of the cross on her forehead. Instead of being grateful, however, she protested vehemently, "No, that doesn't work. I want a real blessing!" I suddenly became aware of the ritualistic quality of my response to her request and said, "Oh, I am sorry,... let me give you a real blessing when we are all together for the prayer service." She nodded with a smile, and I realized that something special was required of me. After the service, when about thirty people were sitting in a circle on the floor, I said, "Janet has asked me for a special blessing. She feels that she needs that now." As I was saying this, I didn't know what Janet really wanted. But Janet didn't leave me in doubt for very long. As soon as I had said, "Janet has asked me for a special blessing," she stood up and walked toward me. I was wearing a long white robe with ample sleeves covering my hands as well as my arms. Spontaneously, Janet put her arms around me and put her head against my chest. Without thinking, I covered her with my sleeves so that she almost vanished in the folds of my robe. As we held each other, I said, "Janet, I want you to know that you are God's Beloved Daughter. You are precious in God's eyes. Your beautiful smile, your kindness to the people in your house and all the good things you do show us what a beautiful human being you are. I know you feel a little low these days and that there is some sadness in your heart, but I want you to remember who you are: a very special person, deeply loved by God and all the people who are here with you."

As I said these words, Janet raised her head and looked at me; and her broad smile showed that she had really heard and received the blessing. When she returned to her place, Jane, another handicapped woman, raised her hand and said, "I want a blessing too." She stood up and, before I knew it, had put her face against my chest. After I had spoken words of blessing to her, many more of the handicapped people followed, expressing the same desire to be blessed. The most touching moment, however, came when one of the assistants, a twenty-four-year-old student, raised his hand and said, "And what about me?" "Sure," I said. "Come." He came, and, as we stood before each other, I put my arms around him and said, "John, it is so good that you are here. You are God's Beloved Son. Your presence is a joy for all of us. When things are hard and life is burdensome, always remember that you are loved with an everlasting love." As I spoke these words, he looked at me with tears in his eyes and then he said, "Thank you, thank you very much."

That evening I recognized the importance of blessing and being blessed and reclaimed it as a true sign of the Beloved. The blessings that we give to each other are expressions of the blessing that rests on us from all eternity. It is the deepest affirmation of our true self. It is not enough to be chosen. We also need an ongoing blessing that allows us to hear in an ever-new way that we belong to a loving God who will never leave us alone, but will remind us always that we are guided by love on every step of our lives. Abraham and Sarah, Isaac and Rebecca, Jacob, Leah and Rachel, they all heard that blessing and so became the fathers and mothers of our faith. They lived their long and often painful journeys without ever forgetting that they were the blessed ones. Jesus, too, heard that blessing after John the Baptist had baptized him in the Jordan. A voice came from heaven saying: "You are my Beloved Son, on you my favor rests." This was a blessing, and it was that blessing that sustained Jesus through all the praise and blame, admiration and condemnation that followed. Like Abraham and Sarah, Jesus never lost the intimate knowledge that he was "the blessed one."

I tell you all of this because I know how moody you and I can be. One day we feel great, the next we feel miserable. One day we are full of new ideas, the next everything looks bleak and dull. One day we think we can take on the whole world, but the next even a little request seems too much for us. These mood swings show that we no longer hear the blessing that was heard by Abraham and Sarah, Isaac and Rebecca, Jacob, Leah and Rachel and Jesus of Nazareth and that we, too, are to hear. When we are thrown up and down by the little waves on the surface of our existence, we become easy victims of our manipulative world, but, when we continue to hear the deep gentle voice that blesses us, we can walk through life with a stable sense of well-being and true belonging.

The feeling of being blessed is not, it seems to me, the feeling that we generally have about ourselves. You have lived many hard moments in your life, moments in which you felt more cursed than blessed. And I can say the same. In fact, I suspect that many people suffer from a deep sense of being cursed. When I simply listen to what people talk about during dinner, in restaurants, during work breaks, I hear much — much blaming and complaining in a spirit of passive resignation. Many people, and we too at times, feel like victims of a world we cannot change, and the daily newspapers certainly don't help much in coping with that feeling. The sense of being cursed often comes more easily than the sense of being blessed, and we can find enough arguments to feed it. We can say: "Look at what is happening in the world: Look at the starving people, the refugees, the prisoners, the sick and the dying....Look at all the poverty, injustice and war. ...Look at the torture, the killings, the destruction of nature and culture....Look at our daily struggles with our relationships, with our work, with our health...." Where, where is the blessing? The feeling of being accursed comes easily. We easily hear an inner voice calling us evil, bad, rotten, worthless, useless, doomed to sickness and death. Isn't it easier for us to believe that we are cursed than that we are blessed?

Still, I say to you, as the Beloved Son of God, you are blessed. Good words are being spoken to you and about you — words that tell the truth. The curses — noisy, boisterous, loud-mouthed as they may be — do not tell the truth. They are lies; lies easy to believe, but lies nevertheless.

Well, if the blessing speaks the truth and the curse speaks lies about who you and I are, we are faced with the very concrete question: How to hear and claim the blessing? If the fact of our blessedness is not just a sentiment, but a truth that shapes our daily lives, we must be able to see and experience this blessing in an unambiguous way. Let me offer you two suggestions for claiming your blessedness. These have to do with prayer and presence.

First of all, prayer. For me personally, prayer becomes more and more a way to listen to the blessing. I have read and written much about prayer, but when I go to a quiet place to pray, I realize that, although I have a tendency to say many things to God, the real "work" of prayer is to become silent and listen to the voice that says good things about me. This might sound self-indulgent, but, in practice, it is a hard discipline. I am so afraid of being cursed, of hearing that I am no good or not good enough, that I quickly give in to the temptation to start talking and to keep talking in order to control my fears. To gently push aside and silence the many voices that question my goodness and to trust that I will hear a voice of blessing... that demands real effort.

Have you ever tried to spend a whole hour doing nothing but listening to the voice that dwells deep in your heart? When there is no radio to listen to, no TV to watch, no book to read, no person to talk to, no project to finish, no phone call to make, how does that make you feel? Often it does no more than make us so aware of how much there is still to do that we haven't yet done that we decide to leave the fearful silence and go back to work! It is not easy to enter into the silence and reach beyond the many boisterous and demanding voices of our world and to discover there the small intimate voice saying: "You are my Beloved Child, on you my favor rests." Still, if we dare to embrace our solitude and befriend our silence, we will come to know that voice. I do not want to suggest to you that one day you will hear that voice with your bodily ears. I am not speaking about a hallucinatory voice, but about a voice that can be heard by the ear of faith, the ear of the inner heart.

Often you will feel that nothing happens in your prayer. You say: "I am just sitting there and getting distracted." But if you develop the discipline of spending one half-hour a day listening to the voice of love, you will gradually discover that something is happening of which you were not even conscious. It might be only in retrospect that you discover the voice that blesses you. You thought that what happened during your time of listening was nothing more than a lot of confusion, but then you discover yourself looking forward to your quiet time and missing it when you can't have it. The movement of God's Spirit is very gentle, very soft — and hidden. It does not seek attention. But that movement is also very persistent, strong and deep. It changes our hearts radically. The faithful discipline of prayer reveals to you that you are the blessed one and gives you the power to bless others.

It might be helpful to offer here a concrete suggestion. One good way to listen is to listen with a sacred text: a psalm or a prayer, for instance. The Hindu spiritual writer Eknath Easwaran showed me the great value of learning a sacred text by heart and repeating it slowly in the mind, word by word, sentence by sentence. In this way, listening to the voice of love becomes not just a passive waiting, but an active attentiveness to the voice that speaks to us through the words of the Scriptures.

I spent many of my half-hours of prayer doing nothing but slowly repeating the prayer of St. Francis: "Lord make me an instrument of your peace. Where there is hatred let me show love...." As I let these words move from my mind to my heart, I began to experience, beyond all my restless emotions and feelings, the peace and love I was asking for in words.

In this way I also had a way to deal with my endless distractions. When I found myself wandering away far and wide, I could always return to my simple prayer and thereby listen again in my heart to the voice I so much wanted to hear.

My second suggestion for claiming your blessedness is the cultivation of presence. By presence I mean attentiveness to the blessings that come to you day after day, year after year. The problem of modern living is that we are too busy — looking for affirmation in the wrong places? — to notice that we are being blessed. Often, people say good things about us, but we brush them aside with remarks such as, "Oh, don't mention it, forget about it, it's nothing..." and so on. These remarks may seem to be expressions of humility, but they are, in fact, signs that we are not truly present to receive the blessings that are given. It is not easy for us, busy people, to truly receive a blessing. Perhaps the fact that few people offer a real blessing is the sad result of the absence of people who are willing and able to receive such a blessing. It has become extremely difficult for us to stop, listen, pay attention and receive gracefully what is offered to us.

Living with people who have a mental handicap makes this clear to me. They have many blessings to offer, but when I am forever busy, forever on the way to something important, how can I receive those blessings? Adam, one of the members of my community, cannot speak, cannot walk alone, cannot eat without help, cannot dress or undress himself, but he has great blessings to offer to those who take the time to be present to him, holding him or just sitting with him. I have yet to meet anyone who spent much time with Adam and didn't feel blessed by him. It is a blessing that comes from simple presence. But you know, too, how hard such simple presence is. There is always so much that still has to be done, so many tasks to finish and jobs to work on that simple presence can easily seem useless and even a waste of our time. But still, without a conscious desire to "waste" our time, it is hard to hear the blessing.

This attentive presence can allow us to see how many blessings there are for us to receive: the blessings of the poor who stop us on the road, the blessings of the blossoming trees and fresh flowers that tell us about new life, the blessings of music, painting, sculpture and architecture — all of that — but most of all the blessings that come to us through words of gratitude, encouragement, affection and love. These many blessings do not have to be invented. They are there, surrounding us on all sides. But we have to be present to them and receive them. They don't force themselves on us. They are gentle reminders of that beautiful, strong, but hidden, voice of the one who calls us by name and speaks good things about us.

Well, I truly hope that these two suggestions, prayer and presence, can help you to claim the blessedness that is yours. I cannot stress enough the importance of making this claim. Not claiming your blessedness will lead you quickly to the land of the cursed. There is little or no neutral territory between the land of the blessed and the land of the cursed. You have to choose where it is that you want to live, and that choice is one that you have to keep making from moment to moment.

Before concluding these thoughts about our being blessed, I must tell you that claiming your own blessedness always leads to a deep desire to bless others. The characteristic of the blessed ones is that, wherever they go, they always speak words of blessing. It is remarkable how easy it is to bless others, to speak good things to and about them, to call forth their beauty and truth, when you yourself are in touch with your own blessedness. The blessed one always blesses. And people want to be blessed! This is so apparent wherever you go. No one is brought to life through curses, gossip, accusations or blaming. There is so much of that taking place around us all the time. And it calls forth only darkness, destruction and death. As the "blessed ones," we can walk through this world and offer blessings. It doesn't require much effort. It flows naturally from our hearts. When we hear within ourselves the voice calling us by name and blessing us, the darkness no longer distracts us. The voice that calls us the Beloved will give us words to bless others and reveal to them that they are no less blessed than we.

You live in New York. I live in Toronto. As you walk down Columbus Avenue and I down Yonge Street, we can have no illusions about the darkness. The loneliness, the homelessness and the addictedness of people are all too visible. Yet all of these people yearn for a blessing. That blessing can be given only by those who have heard it themselves. I now feel ready to write to you about the hardest truth to put into words: the truth of our common brokenness. We are chosen and blessed. When we have truly owned this, have said "Yes" to it, then we can face our own and others' brokenness with open eyes. Let's do that now.

III

BROKEN

The moment has come to talk about our brokenness. You are a broken man. I am a broken man, and
all the people we know or know about are broken.
Our brokenness is so visible and tangible, so concrete and specific, that it is often difficult to believe
that there is much to think, speak or write about
other than our brokenness.

From the moment we met, we spoke about our
brokenness. You wanted something about me for
the Connecticut section of the *New York Times*. I
told you about my writing as a means of dealing with
my loneliness, my sense of isolation, my many fears
and my general sense of insecurity. When the dis-
cussion shifted to you, you spoke of your discontent
with your job, your frustration at not having enough
time or money to write your own novel and your
general confusion as to the course of your life. In the

year that followed our first encounter, we became increasingly open to each other about our suffering and pain. In fact, the sharing of our deep struggles became a sign of our friendship.

You had to live through a painful separation and divorce and I through a long period of depression. You had many disappointments in your work and kept wondering about your true calling in life, while I kept being overwhelmed by the many demands made on my time and energy that often lead me to exhaustion and despair.

Whenever we met again, we became more aware of the brokenness of our lives. There is nothing abnormal about this. When people come together they easily focus on their brokenness. The most-celebrated musical composition, the most-noted painting and sculpture and the most-read books are often direct expressions of the human awareness of brokenness. This awareness is never far beneath the surface of our existence because we all know that none of us will escape death — the most radical manifestation of brokenness.

The leaders and prophets of Israel, who were clearly chosen and blessed, all lived very broken lives. And we, the Beloved Sons and Daughters of God, cannot escape our brokenness either.

There are many things I would like to say to you about our brokenness. But where to begin?

Perhaps the simplest beginning would be to say

that our brokenness reveals something about who we are. Our sufferings and pains are not simply bothersome interruptions of our lives; rather, they touch us in our uniqueness and our most intimate individuality. The way I am broken tells you something unique about me. The way you are broken tells me something unique about you. That is the reason for my feeling very privileged when you freely share some of your deep pain with me, and that is why it is an expression of my trust in you when I disclose to you something of my vulnerable side. Our brokenness is always lived and experienced as highly personal, intimate and unique. I am deeply convinced that each human being suffers in a way no other human being suffers. No doubt, we can make comparisons; we can talk about more or less suffering, but, in the final analysis, your pain and my pain are so deeply personal that comparing them can bring scarcely any consolation or comfort. In fact, I am more grateful for a person who can acknowledge that I am very alone in my pain than for someone who tries to tell me that there are many others who have a similar or a worse pain.

Our brokenness is truly ours. Nobody else's. Our brokenness is as unique as our chosenness and our blessedness. The way we are broken is as much an expression of our individuality as the way we are taken and blessed. Yes, fearsome as it may sound, as the Beloved ones, we are called to claim our unique brokenness, just as we have to claim our unique chosenness and our unique blessedness.

I must try now to get a little closer to our experience of being broken. As I have said already, this is a very personal experience and, in the society in which you and I live, it is generally an experience of inner brokenness — a brokenness of the heart. Although many people suffer from physical or mental disabilities, and although there is a great amount of economic poverty, homelessness and lack of basic human needs, the suffering of which I am most aware on a day-to-day basis is the suffering of the broken heart. Again and again, I see the immense pain of broken relationships between husbands and wives, parents and children, lovers, friends and colleagues. In the Western world, the suffering that seems to be the most painful is that of feeling rejected, ignored, despised and left alone. In my own community, with many severely handicapped men and women, the greatest source of suffering is not the handicap itself, but the accompanying feelings of being useless, worthless, unappreciated and unloved. It is much easier to accept the inability to speak, walk or feed oneself than it is to accept the inability to be of special value to another person. We human beings can suffer immense deprivations with great steadfastness, but when we sense that we no longer have anything to offer to anyone, we quickly lose our grip on life. Instinctively we know that the joy of life comes from the ways in which we live together and that the pain of life comes from the many ways we fail to do that well.

It is obvious that our brokenness is often most painfully experienced with respect to our sexuality. My own and my friends' struggles make it clear how central our sexuality is to the way we think and feel about ourselves. Our sexuality reveals to us our enormous yearning for communion. The desires of our body — to be touched, embraced and safely held — belong to the deepest longings of the heart and are very concrete signs of our search for oneness. It is precisely around this yearning for communion that we experience so much anguish. Our society is so fragmented, our family lives so sundered by physical and emotional distance, our friendships so sporadic, our intimacies so "in-between" things and often so utilitarian, that there are few places where we can feel truly safe. I notice in myself how often my body is tense, how I usually keep my guard up and how seldom I have a complete feeling of being at home. If I then turn to the Toronto suburbs where I live and see the pretentious mega-houses, the ugly shopping malls strewn about to make consumption more efficient and the alluring billboards promising comfort and relaxation in very seductive ways — all of that while forests are demolished, streams dried up, deer and rabbits and birds driven out of my environment — I am not surprised that my body screams for a healing touch and a reassuring embrace. When everything about us overstimulates and overextends our senses and when what is offered to us for the fulfillment of our deeper needs generally has about it a slightly seductive character, it is no wonder that we are plagued by crazy fantasies, wild dreams and disturbing feelings and thoughts. It is where we are most needy and vulnerable that we most experience our brokenness. The fragmentation and commercialization of our milieu makes it nearly impossible to find a place where our whole being — body, mind and heart — can feel safe and protected. Whether we walk on the streets of New York or Toronto, it is hard not to be pulled out of our center and experience, in our own bellies the anguish and agony of our world.

The AIDS epidemic is probably one of the most telling symptoms of our contemporary brokenness. There love and death cling to each other in a violent embrace. Young people, desperate to find intimacy and communion, risk their very lives for it. It seems that there is a cry reverberating through the large, empty spaces of our society: It is better to die than to live in constant loneliness.

Seeing AIDS patients die and seeing the spontaneous generosity with which their friends form community to support them with affection and material and spiritual help, I often wonder if this horrendous illness is not a clear summons to conversion directed to a world doomed by competition, rivalry and ever-increasing isolation. Yes, the AIDS crisis demands a wholly new look at our human brokenness.

How can we respond to this brokenness? I'd like to suggest two ways: first, befriending it and, second, putting it under the blessing. I hope you will be able to practice these ways in your own life. I have tried and try constantly, sometimes with more success than others, but I am convinced that these ways point in the right direction as means for dealing with our brokenness.

The first response, then, to our brokenness is to face it squarely and befriend it. This may seem quite unnatural. Our first, most spontaneous response to pain and suffering is to avoid it, to keep it at arm's length; to ignore, circumvent or deny it. Suffering — be it physical, mental or emotional — is almost always experienced as an unwelcome intrusion into our lives, something that should not be there. It is difficult, if not impossible, to see anything positive in suffering; it must be avoided away at all costs.

When this is, indeed, our spontaneous attitude toward our brokenness, it is no surprise that befriending it seems, at first, masochistic. Still, my own pain in life has taught me that the first step to healing is not a step away from the pain, but a step toward it. When brokenness is, in fact, just as intimate a part of our being as our chosenness and our blessedness, we have to dare to overcome our fear and become familiar with it. Yes, we have to find the courage to embrace our own brokenness, to make our most feared enemy into a friend and to claim it as an intimate companion. I am convinced that healing is often so difficult because we don't want to know the pain. Although this is true of all pain, it is especially true of the pain that comes from a broken heart. The anguish and agony that result from rejection, separation, neglect, abuse and emotional manipulation serve only to paralyze us when we can't face them and keep running away from them. When we need guidance in our suffering, it is first of all a guidance that leads us closer to our pain and makes us aware that we do not have to avoid it, but can befriend it.

I remember vividly the day that I came to your house, and you had just come to the realization that your marriage had come to an end. Your suffering was immense. You saw a life-dream evaporate; you no longer had any sense of a meaningful future; you felt lonely, guilty, anxious, ashamed and deeply betrayed. The pain was etched on your face. It was the hardest moment of your life. I happened to be in New York and dropped in on you. What could I say? I knew that any suggestion that you would get over it, that there were still good things to think about or that things weren't as bad as they seemed, would be completely useless. I knew that the only thing I could do was to be with you, stay with you and somehow encourage you not to run away from your pain, but to trust that you had the strength to stand in it. Now, many years later, you can say that, indeed, you could stand in your pain and grow strong through it. At the moment, it seemed an impossible task, and, still, it was the only task to which I could call you.

My own experience with anguish has been that facing it and living it through, is the way to healing. But I cannot do that on my own. I need someone to keep me standing in it, to assure me that there is peace beyond the anguish, life beyond death and love beyond fear. But I know now, at least, that attempting to avoid, repress or escape the pain is like cutting off a limb that could be healed with proper attention.

The deep truth is that our human suffering need not be an obstacle to the joy and peace we so desire, but can become, instead, the means *to* it. The great secret of the spiritual life, the life of the Beloved Sons and Daughters of God, is that everything we live, be it gladness or sadness, joy or pain, health or illness, can all be part of the journey toward the full realization of our humanity. It is not hard to say to one another: "All that is good and beautiful leads us to the glory of the children of God." But it is very hard to say: "But didn't you know that we all have to suffer and thus enter into our glory?" Nonetheless, real care means the willingness to help each other in making our brokenness into the gateway to joy.

The second response to our brokenness is to put it under the blessing. For me, this "putting of our brokenness under the blessing" is a precondition for befriending it. Our brokenness is often so frightening to face because we live it under the curse. Living our brokenness under the curse means that we experience our pain as a confirmation of our negative feelings about ourselves. It is like saying, "I always suspected that I was useless or worthless, and now I am sure of it because of what is happening to me." There is always something in us searching for an explanation of what takes place in our lives and, if we have already yielded to the temptation to self-rejection, then every form of misfortune only deepens it. When we lose a family member or friend through death, when we become jobless, when we fail an examination, when we live through a separation or a divorce, when a war breaks out, an earthquake destroys our home or touches us, the question "Why?" spontaneously emerges. "Why me?" "Why now?" "Why here?" It is so arduous to live without an answer to this "Why?" that we are easily seduced into connecting the events over which we have no control with our conscious or unconscious evaluation. When we have cursed ourselves or have allowed others to curse us, it is very tempting to explain all the brokenness we experience as an expression or confirmation of this curse. Before we fully realize it, we have already said to ourselves: "You see, I always thought I was no good.... Now I know for sure. The facts of life prove it."

The great spiritual call of the Beloved Children of God is to pull their brokenness away from the shadow of the curse and put it under the light of the blessing. This is not as easy as it sounds. The powers of the darkness around us are strong, and our world finds it easier to manipulate self-rejecting people than self-accepting people. But when we keep listening attentively to the voice calling us the Beloved, it becomes possible to live our brokenness, not as a confirmation of our fear that we are worthless, but as an opportunity to purify and deepen the blessing that rests upon us. Physical, mental or emotional pain lived under the blessing is experienced in ways radically different from physical, mental or emotional pain lived under the curse. Even a small burden, perceived as a sign of our worthlessness, can lead us to deep depression — even suicide. However, great and heavy burdens become light and easy when they are lived in the light of the blessing. What seemed intolerable becomes a challenge. What seemed a reason for depression becomes a source of purification. What seemed punishment becomes a gentle pruning. What seemed rejection becomes a way to a deeper communion.

And so the great task becomes that of allowing

the blessing to touch us in our brokenness. Then our brokenness will gradually come to be seen as an opening toward the full acceptance of ourselves as the Beloved. This explains why true joy can be experienced in the midst of great suffering. It is the joy of being disciplined, purified and pruned. Just as athletes who experience great pain as they run the race can, at the same time, taste the joy of knowing that they are coming closer to their goal, so also can the Beloved experience suffering as a way to the deeper communion for which they yearn. Here joy and sorrow are no longer each other's opposites, but have become the two sides of the same desire to grow to the fullness of the Beloved.

The different twelve-step programs, such as Alcoholics Anonymous, Adult Children of Alcoholics and Overeaters Anonymous, are all ways of putting our brokenness under the blessing and thereby making it a way to new life. All addictions make us slaves, but each time we confess openly our dependencies and express our trust that God can truly set us free, the source of our suffering becomes the source of our hope.

I vividly remember how I had, at one time, become totally dependent on the affection and friendship of one person. This dependency threw me into a pit of great anguish and brought me to the verge of a very self-destructive depression. But from the moment I was helped to experience my interpersonal

addiction as an expression of a need for total surrender to a loving God who would fulfill the deepest
desires of my heart, I started to live my dependency
in a radically new way. Instead of living it in shame
and embarrassment, I was able to live it as an urgent invitation to claim God's unconditional love for
myself, a love I can depend on without any fear.

Well, my dear friend, I wonder if I have helped
you by speaking in this way about our brokenness.
Befriending it and putting it under the blessing do
not necessarily make our pain less painful. In fact,
it often makes us more aware of how deep the
wounds are and how unrealistic it is to expect them
to vanish. Living with mentally handicapped people
has made me more and more aware of how our
wounds are often an essential part of the fabric of
our lives. The pain of parental rejection, the suffering of not being able to marry, the anguish of always
needing help even in the most "normal" things such
as dressing, eating, walking, taking a bus, buying a
gift or paying a bill...none of this brokenness will
ever go away or become less. And still, embracing
it and bringing it into the light of the One who calls
us the Beloved can make our brokenness shine like
a diamond.

Do you remember how, two years ago, we went
to Lincoln Center and heard Leonard Bernstein con-
ducting music by Tschaikovsky? It was a very moving
evening. Later we realized that it was the last time

we were to hear this musical genius. Leonard Bernstein was, no doubt, one of the most influential conductors and composers in introducing me to the beauty and the joy of music. As a teenager, I was completely taken by the enthusiastic way in which he played the role of both conductor and soloist in a performance of the Mozart piano concertos at the Kurhaus Concert Hall in Scheveningen, Holland. When his *West Side Story* appeared on the screen, I found myself humming its captivating melodies for months afterward, returning to the cinema whenever I could.

Watching his expressive face on TV while he directed and explained classical music for children, I realized how much Leonard Bernstein had become my most revered music teacher. It is no surprise, therefore, that his sudden death hit me as that of a very personal friend.

As I write you now about our brokenness, I recall a scene from Leonard Bernstein's *Mass* (a musical work written in memory of John F. Kennedy) that embodied for me the thought of brokenness put under the blessing. Toward the end of this work, the priest, richly dressed in splendid liturgical vestments, is lifted up by his people. He towers high above the adoring crowd, carrying in his hands a glass chalice. Suddenly, the human pyramid collapses, and the priest comes tumbling down. His vestments are ripped off, and his glass chalice falls to the ground and is shattered. As he walks slowly through the debris of his former glory — barefoot, wearing only blue jeans and a T-shirt — children's voices are heard singing, "Laude, laude, laude" — "Praise, praise, praise." Suddenly the priest notices the broken chalice. He looks at it for a long time and then, haltingly, he says, "I never realized that broken glass could shine so brightly."

Those words I will never forget. For me, they capture the mystery of my life, of your life and now, shortly after his death, of Bernstein's own splendid but tragic life.

Before concluding these words about our brokenness, I want to say again something about its implications for our relationships with other people. As I grow older, I am more than ever aware of how little as well as how much we can do for others. Yes indeed, we are chosen, blessed and broken to be given. And it is this I want to speak of now.

IV

GIVEN

We are chosen, blessed and broken so as to be given. The fourth aspect of the life of the Beloved is to be given. For me, personally, this means that it is only as people who are given that we can fully understand our being chosen, blessed and broken. In the giving it becomes clear that we are chosen, blessed and broken not simply for our own sakes, but so that all we live finds its final significance in its being lived for others.

Both of us know from experience the joy that comes from being able to do something for another person. You have done much for me, and I will always be grateful to you for what you have given me. Part of my gratitude, however, is the result of seeing you so happy in giving me so much. It is so much easier to be grateful for a gift given in joy than for a gift given with hesitation or reluctance. Have you ever noticed the joy of a mother when she sees her baby smile? The baby's smile is a gift to the mother who is grateful to see her baby so happy!

What a wonderful mystery this is! Our greatest fulfillment lies in giving ourselves to others. Although it often seems that people give only to receive, I believe that, beyond all our desires to be appreciated, rewarded and acknowledged, there lies a simple and pure desire to give. I remember how I once spent long hours looking in Dutch stores for a birthday gift for my father or mother, simply enjoying being able to give. Our humanity comes to its fullest bloom in giving. We become beautiful people when we give whatever we can give: a smile, a handshake, a kiss, an embrace, a word of love, a present, a part of our life... all of our life. I saw this most movingly on the day you and Robin got married. It was the day on which the grief over the failure of your first marriage came to an end and you were able to fully reclaim the truth that life finds its fulfillment in giving. The afternoon before the wedding, you picked me up from La Guardia Airport, took me to dinner with your mother, your sister, your brother-in-law and your little niece and drove me out to the hotel to spend the night before the celebration. It was a beautiful, sunny May weekend and, although you displayed the usual nervousness of a groom before his wedding, you were peaceful and joyful. Your heart was in the anticipation of your life with Robin. You told me that Robin had given you new confidence in yourself, had taken away your doubts about loving well and finding the perfect job and encouraged you to trust that you would find the best way to use your gifts even when you didn't fit into the traditional slots that society had to offer — and, most importantly, that Robin loved you for who you were and not just for what you would earn or accomplish. You also told me that you were aware of how great a support you had become to Robin. You admired her great commitment as a lawyer for the poor and homeless, her great gifts for defending those who have little voice in our world and her vitality and good humor. But you were also quite aware of how you were giving her something unique that she couldn't give to herself: a home, a place of safety and fruitfulness. Your love for her was so beautiful to see, and I felt so privileged to be invited to be such a close witness to that love.

As we lived the splendid wedding day, with its moving Jewish rituals led by your rabbi friend, Helene Ferris, the joyful garden reception and the gracious dinner, I realized more than ever how true it is that our lives find their fulfillment in giving ourselves to others. That day you gave yourself to Robin and you made it clear that, whatever might happen — be it in your work, with your health or on the economic or political scene — Robin would, from now on, be your first concern.

Since your marriage to Robin was your second marriage and since you had lived through the long loneliness of a divorce, you were quite humble in it all. You knew that nothing good happens automatically and that giving yourself to Robin was a decision that would have to be renewed day after day, especially on days when you experienced distance between yourselves.

I also became deeply aware of how much you need family and friends to surround you with love as you and Robin live out your promises to each other. Your invitation to be so close to you on your wedding day made me aware that you wanted me to be one of the friends who would help you to be faithful, and I experienced that as a joyful responsibility.

It is sad to see that, in our highly competitive and greedy world, we have lost touch with the joy of giving. We often live as if our happiness depended on having. But I don't know anyone who is really happy because of what he or she has. True joy, happiness and inner peace come from the giving of ourselves to others. A happy life is a life for others. That truth, however, is usually discovered when we are confronted with our brokenness.

Reflecting a little more on the way our friendship has grown over the years, I realize that there is a mysterious link between our brokenness and our ability to give to each other. We both went through periods of extreme inner pain. And during those painful times, we often felt that our lives had come to a standstill and that we had nothing to offer; but now, years later, those periods have proven to be the times that made us able to give more instead of less. Our brokenness opened us to a deeper way of sharing our lives and offering each other hope. Just as bread needs to be broken in order to be given, so, too, do our lives. But that clearly does not mean that we should inflict pain on each other or others to make us better givers. Even though a broken glass can shine brightly, only a fool will break glass to make it shine! As mortal people, brokenness is a reality of our existence, and as we befriend it and place it under the blessing, we will discover how much we have to give — much more than we may ever have dreamt.

Isn't a meal together the most beautiful expression of our desire to be given to each other in our brokenness? The table, the food, the drinks, the words, the stories: are they not the most intimate ways in which we not only express the desire to give our lives to each other, but also to do this in actuality? I very much like the expression "breaking bread together," because there the breaking and the giving are so clearly one. When we eat together we are vulnerable to one another. Around the table we can't wear weapons of any sort. Eating from the same bread and drinking from the same cup call us to live in unity and peace. This becomes very visible when there is a conflict. Then, eating and drinking together can become a truly threatening event, then the meal can become the most dreaded moment of the day. We all know about painful silences during dinner. They contrast starkly with the intimacy of eating and drinking together, and the distance between those sitting around the table can be unbearable.

On the other hand, a really peaceful and joyful meal together belongs to the greatest moments of life.

Don't you think that our desire to eat together is an expression of our even deeper desire to be food for one another? Don't we sometimes say: "That was a very nurturing conversation. That was a refreshing time"? I think that our deepest human desire is to give ourselves to each other as a source of physical, emotional and spiritual growth. Isn't the baby at its mother's breast one of the most moving signs of human love? Isn't "tasting" the best word to express the experience of intimacy? Don't lovers in their ecstatic moments experience their love as a desire to eat and drink each other? As the Beloved ones, our greatest fulfillment lies in becoming bread for the world. That is the most intimate expression of our deepest desire to give ourselves to each other.

How can this be done? If our deepest fulfillment comes from being given as a gift for others, how do we go about living such a vision on a day-to-day basis in a society that speaks more about having than giving? I'd like to suggest two directions: giving oneself in life and giving oneself in death.

First of all, our life itself is the greatest gift to give — something we constantly forget. When we think about our being given to each other, what comes immediately to mind are our unique talents: those abilities to do special things especially well. You and I have spoken about this quite often. "What is our unique talent?" we asked. However, when focussing on talents, we tend to forget that our real gift is not so much what we can do, but who we are. The real question is not "What can we offer each other?" but "Who can we be for each other?" No doubt, it is wonderful when we can repair something for a neighbor, give helpful advice to a friend, offer wise counsel to a colleague, bring healing to a patient or announce good news to a parishioner, but there is a greater gift than all of this. It is the gift of our own life that shines through all we do. As I grow older, I discover more and more that the greatest gift I have to offer is my own joy of living, my own inner peace, my own silence and solitude, my own sense of well-being. When I ask myself, "Who helps me most?" I must answer, "The one who is willing to share his or her life with me."

It is worthwhile making a distinction between talents and gifts. More important than our talents are our gifts. We may have only a few talents, but we have many gifts. Our gifts are the many ways in which we express our humanity. They are part of who we are: friendship, kindness, patience, joy, peace, forgiveness, gentleness, love, hope, trust and many others. These are the true gifts we have to offer to each other.

Somehow I have known this for a long time, especially through my personal experience of the enormous healing power of these gifts. But since my coming to live in a community with mentally handicapped people, I have rediscovered this simple truth. Few, if any, of those people have talents they can boast of. Few are able to make contributions to our society that allow them to earn money, compete on the open market or win awards. But how splendid are their gifts! Bill, who suffered intensely as a result of shattered family relationships, has a gift for friendship that I have seldom experienced. Even when I grow impatient or distracted by other people, he remains always faithful and continues to support me in all I do. Linda, who has a speech handicap, has a unique gift for welcoming people. Many who have stayed in our community remember Linda as the one who made them feel at home. Adam, who is unable to speak, walk or eat without help and who needs constant support, has the great gift of bringing peace to those who care for him and live with him. The longer I live in L'Arche, the more I recognize the true gifts that in us, seemingly non-handicapped people, often remain buried beneath our talents. The so-visible brokenness of our handicapped people has, in some mysterious way, allowed them to offer their gifts freely and without inhibition.

More surely than ever before, I know now that we are called to give our very lives to one another and that, in so doing, we become a true community of love.

Secondly, we are called to give ourselves, not only in life, but in death as well. As the Beloved Children of God, we are called to make our death the greatest gift. Since it is true that we are broken so as to be given, then our final brokenness, death, is to become the means to our final gift of self. How can that be true? It seems that death is the great enemy to be evaded for as long as possible. Dying is not something we like to think about or talk about. Still, one of the very few things we can be sure of is that we will die. I am constantly amazed by the lengths to which our society goes to prevent us from preparing ourselves well for death.

For the Beloved Sons and Daughters of God, dying is the gateway to the complete experience of being the Beloved. For those who know they are chosen, blessed and broken to be given, dying is the way to becoming pure gift.

I do not think that you and I have spoken much about death. It seems far away, unreal...something more for others than for us. Even though the media confront us daily with the tragic reality of countless people dying through violence, war, starvation and neglect, and even though we hear regularly that people in our own circle of family and friends have died, we pay very little attention to our own approaching death. In our society we barely take the time to mourn when a friend or family member dies. Everything around us encourages us to keep going "as if nothing has happened." But then we never come in touch with our mortality, and when, finally, we have to face our own approaching death, we try to deny it as long as possible and are perplexed, yes even angry, when we cannot escape it.

Still, as the Beloved, I am called to trust that life is a preparation for death as a final act of giving. Not only are we called to live for others, but also to die for others. How is this possible?

Let me tell you first about three dear friends who have died during the past few months: David Osler, Murray McDonnell and Pauline Vanier. I miss them. Their deaths are a painful loss. Whenever I think of them, I feel the biting pain that they are no longer in their homes with their families and friends. I can no longer call them, visit them, hear their voices or see their faces. I feel immense grief. But I believe deeply that their deaths are more than a loss. Their deaths are also a gift.

The deaths of those whom we love and who love us, open up the possibility of a new, more radical communion, a new intimacy, a new belonging to each other. If love is, indeed, stronger than death, then death has the potential to deepen and strengthen the bonds of love. It was only after Jesus had left his disciples that they were able to grasp what he truly meant to them. But isn't that true for all who die in love?

It is only when we have died that our spirits can completely reveal themselves. David, Murray and Pauline were all beautiful people, but they were also people whose ability to love was limited by their many needs and wounds. Now, after their deaths, the needs and wounds that kept their spirits captive no longer inhibit them from giving their full selves to us. Now they can send us their spirits, and we can live in a new communion with them.

None of this happens without preparation. I know this because I have seen people die in anger and bitterness and with a great unwillingness to accept their mortality. Their deaths became sources of frustration and even guilt for those who stayed behind. Their deaths never became a gift. They had little to send. The spirit has been extinguished by the powers of darkness.

Yes, there is such a thing as a good death. We ourselves are responsible for the way we die. We have to choose between clinging to life in such a way that death becomes nothing but a failure, or letting go of life in freedom so that we can be given to others as a source of hope. This is a crucial choice and we have to "work" on that choice every day of our lives. Death does not have to be our final failure, our final defeat in the struggle of life, our unavoidable fate. If our deepest human desire is, indeed, to give ourselves to others, then we can make our death into a final gift. It is so wonderful to see how fruitful death is when it is a free gift.

In the weeks and months before David died, he spoke to his wife and children about his death. He was able to acknowledge the pain that had existed in their relationship and to affirm the love that was there as well. He could say, "I am sorry" and also, "I thank you." A few moments before he died, no longer able to speak, he stretched out his arms and embraced his wife, Anne, and his children, Susan, Chris and Heather. Then he let go and died. David made his death a gift, and, although his death was a source of deep grief for his family and friends, it is becoming more and more a source of new spiritual energy.

For Murray, who died very suddenly from heart failure, the last five years of his life were a preparation for his death. He had become increasingly vulnerable to his wife, Peggy, his nine children and their families, and to all those he loved. He also had found in himself the courage to make peace with all he had struggled with. His great openness to me, his sincere interest in my life with mentally handicapped people and his generous support of my writing had established a deep bond of friendship between us. I could hardly think of his not being there for me. Still, his death, shocking as it was, became a celebration of love. When his whole family gathered again a year after his death, everyone had beautiful stories to tell about how Murray had given much new life and new hope to all who mourned his leaving.

Pauline Vanier was ninety-three when she died. As the wife of the former governor-general of Canada, she had lived among the great and powerful of this world. But when, after the death of her husband, she joined her son Jean in his community with the weak and powerless, she became grandmother, mother, friend and confidante of many. During the year I lived in her house, she offered me much of her care and shared with me much of her wisdom. Coming to L'Arche will always be connected for me with loving "Mammie." Although I miss her, I know that the fruits of her life will become more and more evident in my life and in the lives of all who were so close to her, and I trust that her spirit, so full of humor and prayer, will continue to guide us.

The death of the Beloved bears fruit in many lives. You and I have to trust that our short little lives can bear fruit far beyond the boundaries of our chronologies. But we have to choose this and trust deeply that we have a spirit to send that will bring joy, peace and life to those who will remember us. Francis of Assisi died in 1226, but he is still very much alive! His death was a true gift, and today, nearly eight centuries later, he continues to fill his brothers and sisters, within and without the Franciscan orders, with great energy and life. He died, but never died. His life goes on bearing new fruit around the world. His spirit keeps descending upon us. More than ever I am convinced that death can, indeed, be chosen as our final gift of life.

You and I have only a short time left to live. The twenty, thirty, forty or fifty years that are still ahead of us will go by very quickly. We can act as if we are to live forever and be surprised when we don't, but we can also live with the joyful anticipation that our greatest desire to live our lives for others can be fulfilled in the way we choose to die. When it is a death in which we lay down our life in freedom, we and all we love will discover how much we have to give.

We are chosen, blessed and broken to be given, not only in life, but in death as well. As the Beloved Children of God, we are called to become bread for each other — bread for the world. This vision gives a new dimension to the Elisha story of the multiplication of the loaves. Elisha said to the servant who came with twenty barley loaves and fresh grain still in the husk: "Give it to the company to eat." When the servant protested: "How can I serve this to a hundred men?" Elisha insisted: "Give it to the company." He served them; they ate and had some left over.

Is this story not the true story of the spiritual life? We may be little, insignificant servants in the eyes of a world motivated by efficiency, control and success. But when we realize that God has chosen us from all eternity, sent us into the world as the blessed ones, handed us over to suffering, can't we, then, also trust that our little lives will multiply themselves and be able to fulfill the needs of countless people? This might sound pompous and self-aggrandizing, but, in truth, the trust in one's fruitfulness emerges from a humble spirit. It is the humble spirit of Hannah who exclaimed in gratitude for the new life born in her: "My spirit exults in God my savior — he has looked upon his lowly handmaid — and done great things for me...from this day forward all generations will call me blessed." The fruitfulness of our little life, once we recognize it and live it as the life of the Beloved, is beyond anything we ourselves can imagine. One of the greatest acts of faith is to believe that the few years we live on this earth are like a little seed planted in a very rich soil. For this seed to bear fruit, it must die. We often see or feel only the dying, but the harvest will be abundant even when we ourselves are not the harvesters.

How different would our life be were we truly

able to trust that it multiplied in being given away! How different would our life be if we could but believe that every little act of faithfulness, every gesture of love, every word of forgiveness, every little bit of joy and peace will multiply and multiply as long as there are people to receive it ... and that — even then — there will be leftovers!

Imagine yourself as being deeply convinced that your love for Robin, your kindness to your friends and your generosity to the poor are little mustard seeds that will become strong trees in which many birds can build their nests! Imagine that, in the center of your heart, you trust that your smiles and handshakes, your embraces and your kisses are only the early signs of a worldwide community of love and peace! Imagine that your trusting that every little movement of love you make will ripple out into ever new and wider circles — just as a little stone thrown into a still pond. Imagine, imagine.... Could you ever be depressed, angry, resentful or vengeful? Could you ever hate, destroy or kill? Could you ever despair of the meaning of your short earthly existence?

You and I would dance for joy were we to know truly that we, little people, are chosen, blessed, and broken to become the bread that will multiply itself in the giving. You and I would no longer fear death, but live toward it as the culmination of our desire to make all of ourselves a gift for others. The fact that we are so far from that state of mind and heart shows only that we are mere beginners in the spiritual life and have not yet fully claimed the full truth of our call. But let us be thankful for every little glimpse of the truth that we can recognize and trust that there is always more to see...always.

Within a few years, we both will be buried or cremated. The houses in which we live will probably still be there, but someone else will live there and most likely know little or nothing about us. But I believe, and I hope you will too, that our brief, easily forgotten journey in this world will continue to give life to people through all times and places. The spirit of love, once freed from our mortal bodies, will blow where it will, even when few will hear its coming and going.

LIVING
as the BELOVED

AS THOSE WHO ARE CHOSEN, blessed, broken and given, we are called to live our lives with a deep inner joy and peace. It is the life of the Beloved, lived in a world constantly trying to convince us that the burden is on us to prove that we are worthy of being loved.

But what of the other side of it all? What of our desire to build a career, our hope for success and fame and our dream of making a name for ourselves? Is that to be despised? Are these aspirations in opposition to the spiritual life?

Some people might answer "Yes" to that question and counsel you to leave the fast pace of the big city and look for a milieu where you can pursue the spiritual life without restraints. But I don't think that that's your way. I don't believe that your place is in a monastery or a community such as L'Arche or the solitude of the countryside. I would say, even, that the city with its challenges is not such a bad place for you and your friends. There is stimulation, excitement, movement and a lot to see, hear, taste and enjoy. The world is only evil when you become its slave. The world has a lot to offer — just as Egypt did for the children of Jacob — as long as you don't feel bound to obey it. The great struggle facing you is not to leave the world, to reject your ambitions and aspirations or to despise money, prestige or success, but to claim your spiritual truth and to live in the world as someone who doesn't belong to it. It is exciting to win a competition, it is interesting to meet influential people, it is inspiring to listen to a concert at Lincoln Center, to see a movie or to visit a new exhibition at the Metropolitan. And what's wrong with good friends, good food and good clothes?

I believe deeply that all the good things our world has to offer are yours to enjoy. But you can enjoy them truly only when you can acknowledge them as affirmations of the truth that you are the Beloved of God. That truth will set you free to receive the beauty of nature and culture in gratitude, as a sign of your Belovedness. That truth will allow you to receive the gifts you receive from your society and celebrate life. But that truth will also allow you to let go of what distracts you, confuses you and puts in jeopardy the life of the Spirit within you.

Think of yourself as having been sent into the world...a way of seeing yourself that is possible if you truly believe that you were loved before the world began...a perception of yourself that calls for a true leap of faith! As long as you live in the world, yielding to its enormous pressures to prove to yourself and to others that you are somebody and knowing from the beginning that you will lose in the end, your life can be scarcely more than a long struggle for survival. If, however, you really want to *live* in the world, you cannot look to the world itself as the source of that life. The world and its strategies may help you to survive for a long time, but they cannot help you live because the world is not the source even of its own life, let alone yours.

Spiritually you do not belong to the world. And this is precisely why you are sent into the world. Your family and your friends, your colleagues and your competitors and all the people you may meet on your journey through life are all searching for more than survival. Your presence among them as the one who is sent will allow them to catch a glimpse of the real life.

Everything changes radically from the moment you know yourself as being sent into this world. Times and spaces, people and events, art and literature, history and science, they all cease to be opaque and become transparent, pointing far beyond themselves to the place from where you come and to where you will return. It is very hard for me to explain to you this radical change because it is a change that cannot be described in ordinary terms; nor can it be taught or practiced as a new discipline of self-knowledge. The change of which I speak is the change from living life as a painful test to *prove* that you deserve to be loved, to living it as an unceasing *"Yes"* to the truth of that Belovedness. Put simply, life is a God-given opportunity to become who we are, to affirm our own true spiritual nature, claim our truth, appropriate and integrate the reality of our being, but, most of all, to say "Yes" to the One who calls us the Beloved.

The unfathomable mystery of God is that God is a Lover who wants to be loved. The one who created us is waiting for our response to the love that gave us our being. God not only says: "You are my Beloved." God also asks: "Do you love me?" and offers us countless chances to say "Yes." That is the spiritual life: the chance to say "Yes" to our inner truth. The spiritual life, thus understood, radically changes everything. Being born and growing up, leaving home and finding a career, being praised and being rejected, walking and resting, praying and playing, becoming ill and being healed — yes, living and dying — they all become expressions of that divine question: "Do you love me?" And at every point of the journey there is the choice to say "Yes" and the choice to say "No."

Once you are able to catch a glimpse of this spiritual vision, you can see how the many distinctions that are so central in our daily living lose their meaning. When joy and pain are both opportunities to say "Yes" to our divine childhood, then they are more alike than they are different. When the experience of being awarded a prize and the experience of being found lacking in excellence both offer us a chance to claim our true identity as the "Beloved" of God, these experiences are more similar than they are different. When feeling lonely and feeling at home both hold a call to discover more fully who the God is whose children we are, these feelings are more united than they are distinct. When, finally, both living and dying bring us closer to the full realization of our spiritual selfhood, they are not the great opposites the world would have us believe; they are, instead, two sides of the same mystery of God's love. Living the spiritual life means living life as one unified reality. The forces of darkness are the forces that split, divide and set in opposition. The forces of light unite. Literally, the word "diabolic" means dividing. The demon divides; the Spirit unites.

The spiritual life counteracts the countless divisions that pervade our daily life and cause destruction and violence. These divisions are interior as well as exterior: the divisions among our most intimate emotions and the divisions among the most widespread social groupings. The division between gladness and sadness within me or the division between the races, religions and cultures around me all find their source in the diabolic forces of darkness. The Spirit of God, the Spirit that calls us the Beloved, is the Spirit that unites and makes whole. There is no clearer way to discern the presence of God's Spirit than to identify the moments of unification, healing, restoration and reconciliation. Wherever the Spirit works, divisions vanish and inner as well as outer unity manifests itself.

What I most want to say is that when the totality of our daily lives is lived "from above," that is, as the Beloved sent into the world, then everyone we meet and everything that happens to us becomes a unique opportunity to choose for the life that cannot be conquered by death. Thus, both joy and suffering become part of the way to our spiritual fulfillment. I found this vision movingly expressed by the novelist Julien Green in a letter to his friend, the French philosopher Jacques Maritain. He writes: " ... when you think of the mystical experience of many saints, you may ask yourself whether joy and suffering aren't aspects of the same phenomenon on a very high level. An analogy, crazy for sure, comes to my mind: extreme cold burns. It seems nearly certain, no, it is certain, that we can only go to God through suffering and that this suffering becomes joy because it finally is the same thing" (*Une grand amitié: Correspondance 1926–1972, Julien Green–Jacques Maritain*, Paris: Gallimard, 1982, p. 282).

Where does all this lead us? I think that it leads us back to the "place" we come from, the "place" of God. We are sent into this world for a short time to say — through the joys and pains of our clock-time — the great "Yes" to the love that has been given to us and in so doing return to the One who sent us with that "Yes" engraved on our hearts. Our death thus becomes the moment of return. But our death can be this only if our whole life has been a journey back to the One from whom we come and who calls us the Beloved. There is such confusion about the idea of a life "hereafter," or "the eternal life." Personally, I do believe deeply in the eternal life, but not simply as a life after our physical death. It is only when we have claimed for ourselves the life of God's Spirit during the many moments of our "chronology" that we expect death to be the door to the fullness of life. Eternal life is not some great surprise that comes unannounced at the end of our existence in time; it is, rather, the full revelation of what we have been and have lived all along. The evangelist John expresses this succinctly when he says: "My dear people, what we are to be in the future has not yet been recorded; all we know is that, when it is recorded, we shall be like him because we shall see him as he really is."

With this vision, death is no longer the ultimate defeat. To the contrary, it becomes the final "Yes" and the great return to where we can most fully become children of God. I don't think that many people look at death this way. Instead of seeing it as a moment of fulfillment, they fear it as the great failure to be kept at bay for as long as possible. All that our society has to say suggests that death is the great enemy who will finally get the better of us against our will and desire. But thus perceived, life is little more than a losing battle, a hopeless struggle, a journey of despair. My own vision and yours too, I hope, is radically different. Even though I often give in to the many fears and warnings of my world, I still believe deeply that our few years on this earth are part of a much larger event that stretches out far beyond the boundaries of our birth and death. I think of it as a mission into time, a mission that is very exhilarating and even exciting, mostly because the One who sent me on the mission is waiting for me to come home and tell the story of what I have learned.

Am I afraid to die? I am every time I let myself be seduced by the noisy voices of my world telling me that my "little life" is all I have and advising me to cling to it with all my might. But when I let these voices move to the background of my life and listen to that small soft voice calling me the Beloved,

I know that there is nothing to fear and that dying is the greatest act of love, the act that leads me into the eternal embrace of my God whose love is everlasting.

EPILOGUE

A Friendship Deepens

After having finished *Life of the Beloved,* I sent it to Fred, anxiously wondering whether I had been able to respond to his request: "Say something about the Spirit that my secular friends and I can hear." I had tried to speak from my heart to his heart, from my own most personal experience to his, from my true self to his true self. I was very curious to know whether I had succeeded.

Shortly after Fred had received the text, he called me and offered to come to Toronto to spend a few days in the community and talk about "the life of the Beloved." When he came, we became aware that the past decade had brought us to a place much more solid than when we first met. I had found a true home in L'Arche, and Fred was happily married, waiting for his first child and satisfied in his job. He had published two books for teenagers, one about the Gulf War and another about losing a parent, and he was preparing a book in which leaders and experts in fields as different as politics, the arts, literature and sports recommend the best books to read. He was even using his early morning hours to work on a novel! This dream of becoming a writer has, in fact, come true, though in a way different from what he had anticipated.

Both of us had grown a lot. We had become less insecure and more rooted. But we also had become more aware of the distance between us. During our long conversations about the text of this book, it became increasingly clear that, although Fred had many good things to say about my words to him, I had not been able to do what he had hoped for. He had shown the manuscript to two of his friends and it was clear that neither of them had been deeply touched. As we talked more, Fred convinced me that this book was not as radically different from my previous books as I had assumed. Fred had always liked my writing, but never as writing that spoke directly to his own needs. For him, it was writing for the "converted" and not for truly secular people. He felt this book wasn't very different in this respect.

I was very disappointed that the gap between us, when it concerned the spiritual life, was so much greater than I had thought. I had so much hoped that, after our long years as friends, I would have been able to find the words to bridge that gap. I had so much hoped that I would have been able to speak to Fred and his friends in a way that would open in them a true desire to develop a life in the Spirit.

Why had I not been able to speak to the most basic concerns of Fred and his friends? Fred was very gentle about it, very aware of my sensitivities, but also very clear. He said, "Although it is clear that you try to write for me and my friends from your own center and although you express to us what is most precious to you, you do not realize how far we are from where you are. You speak from a context and tradition that is alien to us, and your words are based on many presuppositions that we don't share with you. You are not aware of how truly secular we are. Many, many questions need to be answered before we are able to be fully open to what you say about the life of the Beloved."

It wasn't easy to hear this criticism, but I wanted to listen to it in a non-defensive way so that I could discover in my own heart where I was being challenged. My attempt had been to be a "witness of God's love" to a secular world, but I had sounded like someone who is so excited about the art of sailing that he forgets that his listeners have never seen lakes or the sea, not to mention sailboats!

Fred tried to explain the problem. "Long before you start speaking about being the Beloved and becoming the Beloved, you have to respond to some very fundamental questions such as: Who is God? Who am I? Why am I here? How can I give my life meaning? How do I get faith? When you do not help us to answer these questions, your beautiful meditations on being and becoming the Beloved remain dreamlike for us."

Fred said many other things, but the main response to all I had written was that I had not truly entered into the secular mentality. When I am honest with my experiences among my nephews and nieces in Holland, my business friends in Canada and the United States, and my many correspondents from all over the world, I have to confess that Fred's criticism would most likely be affirmed by many of them. The issue is no longer how to express the mystery of God to people who are no longer accustomed to the traditional language of Church or Synagogue; the issue is whether there is anything in our world that we can call "sacred." Is there, among the things we do, the people we know, the events we read about in the newspapers or watch on TV, someone or something that transcends it all and has the inner quality of sacredness, of being holy, worthy of adoration and worship?

Fred was quite willing to say that, with the disappearance of the sacred from our world, the human imagination had been impoverished and that many people live with a sense of loss, even emptiness. But where and how can we rediscover the sacred and give it the central place in our lives? I am quite aware now that, in this book, I have not adequately responded to this question.

Could I have done so? Should I have done so? Fred and I spent a few days together in the Daybreak community. As we visited the different homes where mentally handicapped people and their assistants share their lives together, I became increasingly aware that I can speak and write only about ideas and visions that are anchored in my own daily experiences. And these experiences are completely pervaded with the knowledge of God's presence. Would I be able to step out of that God-centered reality and respond to those who say: "Do I really need God to live, to be happy, to enjoy life, to fulfill my deepest desires? Do I need faith to live a decent and creative life?"

I feel within myself a deep-rooted resistance to proving anything to anybody. I don't want to say: "I will show you that you need God to live a full life." I can only say: "For me, God is the one who calls me the Beloved, and I have a desire to express to others how I try to become more fully who I already am." But beyond that I feel very poor and powerless.

However, all of this does not mean that Fred's response to this book doesn't hold a tremendous challenge for me. It is the challenge to explore my own inner solidarity with the secular world. Although I live in a Christian community and feel quite responsible for protecting and nurturing the sacred in our common life, I am surrounded, within as well as without the boundaries of our community, by the secular world. But more than that, I know that as much as I focus in my life on the sacred, I am also a very secular person. The questions that Fred raises are not alien to me. In fact, the more I enter into an intimate dialogue with the secular world, the more I discover my own secularity and the more I can see that Fred and his friends are not as far away from me as I might have thought.

Maybe the great challenge is to trust so much in God's love that I don't have to be afraid to enter fully into the secular world and speak there about faith, hope and love. Maybe the place where the gap has to be bridged is within me. Maybe the distinction between secular and sacred can be bridged when they have both been identified as aspects of every person's experience of being human. Maybe I don't have to become an apologist for God's existence and the religious meaning of life in order to respond to Fred's criticism... at this moment I can say no more than that.

After Fred's visit to Daybreak, I was left with the question: What to do with this book? Forget about it, rewrite it, publish it as it is? For a long time I was quite confused.

Then something unexpected happened. Having sent it to Gordon Cosby and Diana Chambers of the Servant Leadership School of the Church of the Saviour in Washington, D.C., I received a very encouraging reply. They wrote me that this text had helped them more than previous ones and had inspired them to offer a new course in "The Life of the Beloved." Also, Bart Gavigan of the South Park Community in England responded very enthusiastically to the text. Gordon, Diana and Bart all urged me not to change much, but just to trust that what is there will bear fruit. "What about Fred?" I asked. "Well," they answered, "you might not have been able to write all that Fred needs to hear, but Fred certainly enabled you to write what we need to hear! Couldn't you just be happy with that?"

Here the real irony of writing hit me. I had tried so hard to write something for secular people, and the ones who were most helped by it were searching Christians in Washington and London. I suddenly realized that without Fred I would never have found the words that were so helpful to believers. For me, there is more than an irony here. It is the mystery of God using his secular friends to instruct his disciples.

It was this realization that finally made me decide not to write a new book, but to trust that what is here should be published and that what is not here may one day find an authentic form of expression.

OUR GREATEST GIFT

Our
Greatest
Gift

A Meditation on
Dying and Caring

Henri J. M. Nouwen

Hodder & Stoughton
LONDON SYDNEY AUCKLAND

To Marina Nouwen - San Giorgi

Her courage and joy were a great inspiration to me. She died in the early morning of May 8th, 1993. May this book honour her.

CONTENTS

Acknowledgments   9
PROLOGUE Befriending Death   11

INTRODUCTION Grace Hidden In
    Powerlessness   17

PART I DYING WELL   25

Chapter 1   We Are the Children of God   29
Chapter 2   We Are Each Other's Brothers
    and Sisters   39
Chapter 3   We Are Parents of Generations
    to Come   49

PART II CARING WELL   63

Chapter 4   You Are a Child of God   67
Chapter 5   You Are Brothers and Sisters of
    Each Other   81

Contents

**Chapter 6   You Are the Parents of Generations
     to Come   95**

CONCLUSION   The Grace of the
     Resurrection   111

EPILOGUE   Death: A Loss and A Gift   121

ACKNOWLEDGEMENTS

This little book would never have been written without the warm friendship and generous hospitality of my German friends Franz and Reny Johna. In their home I found not only a quiet place to write, but also lively company to discuss my thoughts and bounce off my ideas. My gratitude to them is deep and lasting.

I also want to thank all the friends who are mentioned in this book. Not only did they allow me to write about them, but many took the time to read the manuscript critically and make suggestions for changes and additions.

A special word of thanks goes to my secretary Kathy Christie for typing and retyping the text and for offering me much needed encouragement and support during the final phases of this book. I am also very grateful to Conrad Wieczorek, Bart Gauigan, and John Shopp for their advice and careful editing work.

Our Greatest Gift

Finally, I want to express my deep gratitude to Peggy McDonnell, her family and friends. Their loyal friendship, and generous financial support, in memory of Murray McDonnell, have allowed me to find time and space to keep writing in the midst of a very busy life.

Henri J. M. Nouwen

PROLOGUE

Befriending Death

On December 31, 1992 at 3.00 p.m., Maurice Gould died. He died in York Central Hospital in Richmond Hill, near Toronto, after a long struggle with Alzheimer's disease.

Maurice — 'Moe' as we called him — had been a member of L'Arche. Founded in 1964 by the Canadian, Jean Vanier, L'Arche is a world-wide network of communities, where people with mental disabilities and their assistants create home for one another. It was in the L'Arche Daybreak community in Toronto, that Maurice had made his home for fourteen years.

He was known for his joyfulness, gentleness and love of home. The countless people who met him over the years speak about him with much endearment. Somehow his handicap — Down's Syndrome — seems only the other side of his great gift: to give and receive love.

11

Our Greatest Gift

During the last days of Moe's life, I was in Freiburg, Germany. Daybreak had sent me there to take a few months away from my pastoral work in the community, to focus exclusively on my writing. When Nathan Ball, the Director of our community, called me and told me about Moe's death, I knew at once that I must return to Toronto as soon as possible to be with Moe's family and many friends to experience with them the sorrow of his leaving, as well as the joy of the fulfillment of his fifty-eight years of life.

During the long trip home, I thought a great deal about life and death and began wondering how our dying can be as much our own as our living.

As the Air Canada plane took me from Frankfurt over Germany, Holland, England, the Atlantic Ocean and Nova Scotia to Toronto, I had ample time to think about dying: Maurice's dying, my own dying and the dying of so many people day after day all over the world.

Is death something so terrible and absurd that we are better off not thinking or talking about it? Is death such an undesirable part of our existence that we are better off acting as if it were not real? Is death such an absolute end of all our thoughts and actions that we simply cannot face it? Or is it possible to befriend our dying and death gradually and live towards it with open eyes and open arms, trusting that there is nothing to fear. Is it possible to prepare for our death with the same attentive-ness as our parents prepared themselves for our birth? Can we wait for our death as for a friend who wants to welcome us home?

During the eight-and-a-half-hour flight, I thought not only about Maurice, but also about my dying friends and my aging father. Less than two months earlier, on November 24, I was with Rick in Bethany House, the Catholic Worker house in Oakland, California. Rick has AIDS and knows that he has only a short time left to live. As I sat on his bed and held his hand, he said: 'What can I still do in the months that are left to me; ... my friend, whom I love so much, can make all sorts of plans for his future, but I have no future any more.' Tears flowed from his eyes as he tightened his grip on my hand.

And then I thought of Marina, my sister-in-law, who has struggled for five full years with intestinal cancer, has survived three horrendous surgeries and has finally, when all further therapy proved useless, allowed things to take their natural course. She has spoken openly about her death to her doctors, to the nurses, to her many close friends, to her mother, to her husband Paul and to me. And in her poems she expresses her feelings about her approaching death, even while those around her hardly dare to mention it in her presence.

Meanwhile, my father in Holland will celebrate his

ninetieth birthday within ten days. He is full of energy, still writing, still lecturing, still making new plans, but to me he says: 'Son, my body is spent, my eyes are no longer able to focus, my stomach doesn't tolerate much food any more, and my heart is very, very weak.'

People are dying ... not just the few I know, but countless people everywhere, every day, every hour. Dying is the most general human event, something we all have to do. But do we do it well? Is our death more than an unavoidable fate that we simply wished would not be there, or can it somehow become an act of fulfillment, perhaps more human than any other human act.

When I arrived at Terminal II at Pearson International Airport in Toronto, Nathan Ball, the director of Daybreak and a close friend, was waiting for me. In the car he told me about Moe's death. Family and friends had been with him during his last hours. Both sadness and gladness were there. A beautiful friend had left us, a long suffering had come to a gentle end. 'Moe was so much loved by everyone,' Nathan said. 'We will miss him, but it was time for him to go.'

The days that followed were days full of sorrow and joy. Moe was dead, but it seemed as if new life became immediately visible. Telephone calls were made to friends far and wide; letters were written, but most of all, people came together to pray, to eat, to tell stories, to look at pictures ... to remember with smiles and tears. Of all the days that I have lived at Daybreak these days belong to the most intimate, the most uniting and, in a strange way, the most sacred. A man who, through his fragility and weakness, had helped us create community during his life, did so even more through his death. As we came together in our chapel, visited the funeral home, sang and spoke in gratitude in the Anglican Church of Richmond Hill and carried the coffin to the grave in King City's cemetery, there was a deep sense that, not only life leads to death, but also that death leads to new life. The spirit of gentleness and kindness that surrounded and pervaded our conversation, the spirit of forgiveness and healing that touched each of us and, most of all, the spirit of unity and communion that bound us together in a new way — that spirit was gratefully received as a gift from Moe who was dead, and yet very much alive!

On the evening before my return to Europe to celebrate my father's birthday and to continue my writing in Freiburg, I had dinner with Nathan and Sue Mosteller, a friend and long-time member of Daybreak. During the meal, Nathan asked me: 'Where and how do you want to die?' The question was raised in a very gentle way. It was a question that came from the new awareness that not only Moe had died, but that we too would soon die. Out of that awareness we had to ask ourselves: 'Are we preparing ourselves for our deaths or are we going to keep busy until we can't be busy any longer? Are we helping each other to die or are we simply going to assume that we are always going to be there for each other? Is our death going to give new life, new hope, new faith to our friends, or is it going to be no more than another cause for sadness?' The main question is not: 'How much will we still be able to do during the few years we have left to live?', but: 'How can we prepare ourselves for our deaths in such a way that our dying will be a new way for us to send our and God's spirit to those we have loved and who have loved us?'

Nathan's question: 'How and where do you want to die?' brought me face to face with the great challenge: not only to live well, but to die well.

The next day, as we drove to the airport, Nathan thanked me for returning for Moe's funeral and wished me a happy celebration of my father's birthday and a creative month of writing in Freiburg. Flying to Amsterdam, I realized that I knew better than before what I had to write about. I had to write about befriending my death, so that my death can become my best gift to the world I love so much.

Now — after many celebrations in Holland and a long train-ride through Germany — I am alone again in my little, peaceful and solitary apartment in Freiburg. What better place than this in which to befriend death.

INTRODUCTION

Grace Hidden in Powerlessness

It has never been easy for me to find a quiet place to write. I have gone to convents, monasteries, retreat centers and even tried to stay home with the door closed. But wherever I searched for solitude, I soon became entangled again in the daily events of my surroundings. My own restlessness, my need for companionship, my fear of rejection and abandonment made me flee solitude as soon as I had found it. The resistance to solitude proved as strong as my desire for it. Over and over again I found excuses to talk to people, give conferences, preach sermons, preside at liturgies, join in celebrations or hang around in libraries; in short: excuses not to be alone.

Still, I always knew that one day, I would have to find the courage to go beyond my fear and trust that, in solitude, I would discover my true teacher, who would give me the words that I must write.

Now I have my chance. Franz and Reny Johna, my friends in Freiburg, have offered me the third story of their three-story house in the Schubert Strasse. The first serves as their own home; the second is rented to an elderly couple; the third is kept free for their two children, Robert and Irene. Robert, however, has moved to the United States, where he specializes in internal medicine, and Irene has moved to Frankfurt where she works for the Bundesbank. 'You can have the third-story apartment,' Franz and Reny said to me. 'It is a true hermitage, away from people and the events of every day and definitely noise- and light-proof.' Indeed, the third-story apartment of Franz and Reny's house is the ideal place for a 'city-hermit.' It has everything a solitary person can desire: three small rooms, a kitchen and a bathroom.

So, now I have what I always dreamt of having: complete silence, complete solitude. When I let down the window blinds, my bedroom is pitch dark, and not even the sound of a passing car can be heard. All becomes completely still.

And this stillness is purifying. Because, strange as it may seem, the outer quietude quickly reveals the inner restlessness. What am I going to do when there is nothing to do? What am I going to do when there is no one demanding my attention or inviting me to do something or making me feel valuable?

Introduction

Without phone calls, letters, meetings ... the minutes, hours and days start stretching themselves out into horizonless deserts of solitude.

But is this not the most blessed place in which to befriend my death? Is this not the place where the outer silence can gradually lead me to an inner silence and where I can embrace my own mortality? Yes, silence and solitude invite me to a gradual letting go of all the outer voices that give me a sense of well-being among my fellow humans and to trust in the inner voice that reveals to me my true name. Silence and solitude call me to detach myself from the scaffolding of daily life and to discover if there is anything there that can stand on its own when the traditional support systems have been pulled away.

Sitting alone in my little hermitage, I realize how unprepared I am to die. The silence and solitude of this comfortable apartment are sufficient to make me aware of my unwillingness to let go of life. Nevertheless, I will have to die soon. The ten, twenty, or thirty years left to me will fly by quickly. Gradually, my body will lose its strength and my mind its flexibility; I will lose family and friends; I will become less relevant to society and be forgotten by most; I will have to depend increasingly on the help of others; and, in the end, I will have to let go of everything and be carried into the completely unknown.

Am I willing to make that journey? Am I willing to

let go of whatever power I have left; to unclench my fists and trust in the grace hidden in complete powerlessness? I don't know. I really don't know. It seems impossible, since everything alive in me protests against this journey into nothingness. But I do know that the small silence and solitude of my apartment in Freiburg is as close as I will ever come to an opportunity to explore my ability to surrender to death.

Somehow, I believe that this lonely task to befriend my death is not simply a task that serves me, but also a task that may serve others. I have lived my whole life with the desire to help others in their journey, but I have always realized that I had little else to offer than my own. How will I ever be able to announce joy, peace, forgiveness and reconciliation unless they are part of my own flesh and blood? I have always wanted to be a good shepherd for others, but I have always known, too, that *good* shepherds are those who lay down their own lives — their pains and joys, their doubts and hopes, their fears and their love — for their friends.

In my sixties, trying to come to terms with my own mortality, I trust that, like everything else I have lived, my attempt to befriend my death will be good, not only for me, but also for those others who face a similar challenge. I want to die well, but I desire also to help others to die well. In this way I am not alone in my little third-floor apartment in the Schubert Strasse in Freiburg. In fact I am surrounded by a world of people who are dying and who hope to die well. I want my silence and solitude to be for my friends and the friends of my friends. I want my desire to embrace my own mortality to help others embrace theirs. I want my little hermitage to be truly in and for the world.

There are five weeks ahead of me in this sanctuary. Five weeks in which to pray, to think and to write about dying and death – my own as well as others'. There are two sides to my task. First of all, I have to discover what it means to befriend my own death, and second, I have to discover how I can help others in befriending their own. The inner life is always a life for others. When I myself am able to befriend death, I will be able to help others do the same. That's the 'work' of this little book. Therefore, I want first to write about dying well, then about caring well.

PART I
DYING WELL

Close to the Heart

As children, we need parents, teachers and friends to teach us the meaning of our lives, but once we have grown up, we are on our own. Then, we ourselves become the main source of knowledge, and what we say to others about life and death has to come from what is truly our own. Great thinkers and great saints have written and spoken about dying and death, but their words remain uniquely theirs. I have to find my own, so that what I say really comes from the depth of my own experience. Although that experience is deeply influenced by many people, it is an experience that nobody else has had. In this lies its power, but in this too, lies its weakness. I have to trust that my own experience of mortality will give me words that can speak to others struggling to give meaning to their own lives and deaths. I also have to accept that many will not be able to respond to what I have to say, simply because they cannot see or feel the connections between their lives and mine.

In the first three chapters of this book I will deal with dying well. I want to explore in my own innermost being what it means that we human beings are children of God, brothers and sisters of each other, and parents of generations to come.

I want to stay very close to my own heart, listening carefully to what I have heard and felt. I also want to stay close to the hearts of those whose joys and pains are touching me most at this time of my life. Most of all, I want to stay close to the heart of Jesus, whose life and death are the main source for understanding and living my own.

I

We Are the Children of God

When I became sixty, the Daybreak community gave me a big party. More than one hundred people came together to celebrate. John Bloss was there and, as always, eager to play an active role. John is full of good thoughts, but his handicap makes it painfully difficult for him to express them in words. Still he loves to speak, especially when he has a captive audience.

With everyone sitting in a large circle, Joe, the master of ceremonies, said: 'Well John, what do you have to say to Henri today?' John, who loves the theatrical, got up, put himself in the center of the circle, pointed to me and began to search for words. 'You ... you ... are,' he said with a big grin on his face. 'You ... you ... are ... uh ... uh ...' Everyone looked at him with great expectation as he tried to get his words out while pointing ever more directly at me. 'You ... you ... are ... uh ...

uh.' And then like an explosion the words came out. 'An old man!' Everybody burst out in a roar of laughter, and John basked in the success of his performance.

Well, that said it all. I had become 'an old man.' Very few people would say it so directly, and most would continue with qualifications about, 'still looking young, still so full of energy and so on and on', but John said it simply and truthfully: 'You are an old man.'

It seems fair to say that between the ages of one and thirty, people are considered young; between thirty and sixty they are considered middle-aged, and after sixty, they are considered old. But when you, yourself, are 'suddenly' sixty, you don't feel old. At least I don't! My teenage years seem only a short time ago, my years of studying and teaching feel like yesterday, and my seven years at Daybreak feel like seven days!

Thinking of myself as an 'old man' does not come spontaneously. It has to be announced to me loud and clear. I vividly remember listening to a student who spoke to me about his father. 'My dad doesn't understand me,' he said. 'He is so bossy; he always wants to be right; he never allows any room for my ideas... It is very difficult to be with him.' Trying to comfort him, I said: 'Well, my dad is not very different from yours. He also is quite authoritarian ... but you know ... that's the older generation!' Then he said: 'Yes, my dad is already forty!' As he said this, I suddenly realized that I was speaking to someone who could have been my grandson!

Indeed, I somehow keep forgetting that I have become old and that young people regard me as an old man. It helps to look at myself in a mirror once in a while. Gazing at my own face, I see both my mother and my father when they were sixty years old, and I remember how I thought of them as old people.

Being an 'old man' means being close to death. In the past, I often tried to figure out if I could still double the years I had lived. When I was twenty, I was sure that I would live at least another twenty years. When I was thirty, I trusted that I would easily reach sixty. When I was forty, I wondered if I would make it to eighty. And when I turned fifty, I realized that only a very few make it to one hundred. But now, as I am sixty, I am sure that I have gone far past the half-way point and that my death is a lot closer to me than my birth.

Old men and old women must prepare for death. But how do we prepare ourselves well? For me, the first task is to become a child again — to reclaim my childhood. This might sound the opposite of our natural desire to maintain a maximum of independence. Nevertheless, becoming a child — entering our second childhood — is essential for dying a good death. Jesus speaks about this second childhood when he says: 'Unless you change and become like little children, you will never enter the kingdom of heaven' (Matt. 18:3).

And what characterizes this second childhood? It has to do with a new dependency. For the first twenty or so years of our lives we are dependent on our parents, teachers and friends. Forty years later, we again become increasingly dependent. The younger we are, the more people we need to live, and the older we become, the more people we will need again to live. Life is lived from dependency to dependency.

That's the mystery that God reveals to us through Jesus, whose life is a journey from the manger to the cross. Born in complete dependence on those who surrounded him, he died as the passive victim of other people's actions and decisions. It was the journey from the first to the second childhood. He came as a child and died as a child, and he lived his life so that we might claim and reclaim our own childhood and thus make our death — as he did — into a new birth.

I have been blessed with an experience that made all of this very clear to me. A few years ago, when I was hit by a car and brought to the hospital with a ruptured spleen, the doctor told me that she wasn't sure that I would make it through surgery. I did — but the hours lived before and after the operation allowed me to get in touch with my childhood as never before. Bound with straps on a table that looked like a cross and surrounded by masked figures, I suddenly experienced my complete dependency. Not only did I realize that I was fully dependent on the skills of an unknown medical team, but also that my deepest being was a dependent being. I knew with a certainty that had nothing to do with any particular human insight that, whether I survived the surgery or not, I was safely held in a divine embrace and would certainly live.

While being forced by a freak accident into a childlike state in which I needed to be cared for as a helpless infant, I was led to an experience that offered me an immense sense of safety — the experience of being a child of God. All at once I knew that all human dependencies are embedded in a divine dependency and that this divine dependency makes dying part of a greater and vaster way of living. This experience was so real, so basic and so all-pervasive that it changed radically my sense of self and affected profoundly my state of consciousness for years to follow.

There is a strange paradox here: dependency on people often leads to slavery, but dependency on God, when lived in trust, leads to freedom. When we know that God holds us safe — whatever happens — we don't have to fear anything or anyone but can walk through life with great confidence. This is a radical perspective, since we are so accustomed to thinking about the ways in which people are oppressed and exploited as signs of their dependency and therefore can only perceive of true freedom as the result of independence. However, there is another way of thinking about all of this. When we claim our most intimate dependency on God, not as a curse but as a gift, then we can discover the 'freedom of the children of God.' It is this deep inner freedom that allows us to confront our enemies, throw off the yoke of oppression and build social and economic structures that allow us to live as brothers and sisters, children of the one God whose name is love. This, I believe, is the way Jesus speaks about freedom. It is freedom rooted in being a child of God.

We are very fearful people. We are afraid of conflict, war, an uncertain future, illness and, most of all, death. This fear takes away our freedom and gives our society the power to manipulate us with threats and promises. But when we can reach beyond our fears to the One who loves us with a love that was there before we were born and will be there after we have died, then oppression, persecution and even death will be unable to take away our freedom. Once we have come to the deep inner knowledge — a knowledge more of the heart than of the mind — that we are born out of love and will die into love, that every part of our being is deeply rooted in love and that this love is our true Father and Mother, then all forms of evil, illness and death lose their final power over us and become painful, but also hopeful reminders of our true divine childhood. It is this experience of the complete freedom of the children of God that the apostle Paul expresses when he writes: 'I am certain of this: neither death nor life, nor angels, nor principalities, nothing already in existence and nothing still to come, nor any power, nor the heights nor the depths, nor any created thing whatever, will be able to come between us and the love of God, known to us in Christ Jesus' (Rom. 8:38).

So the first task in preparing ourselves for death is to claim the freedom of the children of God and in so doing, strip death of any further power over us. The word 'child' has its problems. It suggests littleness, weakness, naïveté and immaturity. But when I say that we must grow into a second childhood, I am not thinking about a second immaturity. To the contrary, I am thinking about the maturity of the sons and daughters of God. Sons and daughters who are chosen to inherit the Kingdom. There is nothing little, weak or naïve about being a child of God. In fact, it is an election that allows us to keep our heads erect in the presence of God even while we walk through a world falling apart on every side.

As sons and daughters of God, we can walk through the gates of death with the self-confidence of heirs. Paul again proclaims this loudly as he says: 'All who are guided by the Spirit of God are sons [and daughters] of God: for what you received was not the spirit of slavery to bring you back into fear; you have received the spirit of adoption, enabling us to cry out, "Abba, Father." The Spirit himself joins with our spirit to bear witness that we are children of God. And if we are children, then we are heirs, heirs of God and joint-heirs with Christ, provided we share his suffering, so as to share his glory' (Rom. 8: 14—17).

This is not the voice of a small, timid child. This is the voice of a spiritually mature person who knows that he is in the presence of God and for whom complete dependency on God has become the source of his strength, the basis of his courage and the secret of his true inner freedom.

I would like to conclude this chapter with a small story recently told me by a friend. It is a story about twins, sister and brother, talking to each other in the womb. The little sister said to her little brother: 'I believe that there is life after birth!' Her brother protested vehemently: 'No, no, this is all there is. This is a dark and cosy place, and we have nothing else to do but to cling on to the cord that feeds us.' But the little girl insisted: 'There must be something more than this dark place, there must be something else where there is light and freedom to move.' Still she could not convince her twin brother. Then ... after some silence, she said hesitantly: 'I have something else to say, and I am afraid you won't believe that either, but I think there is a mother!' Her little brother now became furious: 'A mother, a mother,' he shouted, 'what are you talking about? I have never seen a mother and neither have you. Who put that idea in your head? As I told you, this place is all we have! Why do you always want more. This is not such a bad place after all. We have all we need, so let's be content.' The little sister was quite overwhelmed by her brother's response and for a while didn't dare to say anything more, but she couldn't let go of her thoughts, and since there was nobody else to speak to but her twin brother, she finally said: 'Don't you feel these squeezes every once in a while? They really are quite unpleasant and sometimes even painful.' 'Yes,' he answered, 'what's special about that?' 'Well,' the sister said, 'I think that these squeezes are there to get us ready for another place, much more beautiful than this, where we will see our mother face to face! Don't you think that's exciting!'

Her little brother didn't answer. He was fed up with the foolish talk of his sister and felt that the best thing was simply to ignore her and hope that she would leave him alone.

This little story may help us to think about our death in a new way. We can live as if this life were all we had and that death is simply absurd and that we had better not talk about it; or we can choose to claim our divine childhood and trust that death is the painful, but blessed passage that will bring us face to face with our God.

2

We Are Each Other's Brothers and Sisters

Two of the greatest joys experienced are: that of being different from others and that of being the same as others. The first joy I experienced while watching the 1992 summer Olympics on television in Barcelona. The joy of those who stood on the rostrum and received their bronze, silver or gold medals was the direct result of their ability to run faster, jump higher or throw farther than others. The difference from others might have been extremely small, but it made all the difference. It was the difference between defeat and victory, rueful tears and ecstatic joy. This is the joy of the hero and the star. It is the joy that comes from successfully competing, winning the prize, receiving the honor and walking into the limelight.

I know that joy myself. I know it from getting an

award at school, from being chosen the leader of my class, from receiving tenure at the university, from seeing books published and from receiving honorary degrees. I know the immense satisfaction that comes from being considered different from others. It dispels many self-doubts and bestows an immense self-confidence. It is the joy of having 'made it'; it is the joy of being recognized for the difference you make. We all wait for that joy somewhere, somehow ... but still, it remains the joy of the one who said: 'I thank you God, that I am not like everyone else' (Luke 18: 11–12).

There is, however, another joy: harder to describe, but easier to find. It is the joy of being the brother or sister of all people.

Although this joy is closer at hand than the joy of being different and, therefore, more accessible, it is not an obvious joy, and only a few people ever truly find it. It is the joy of being a part of that vast variety of people – of all ages, colors and religions – who together form the human family. It's that immense joy of being a member of the human race.

At several times in my life, I have tasted that joy. Most acutely in 1964 when I drove my little red Volkswagen to Alabama and walked with thousands of people from Selma to Montgomery in a civil rights march led by Martin Luther King. During that march, I had an experience of joy that I will never forget. I had come by myself. Nobody knew me, nobody had ever heard of me, but when we walked together and put our arms around each other's shoulders and sang: 'We shall overcome one day,' I knew a joy such as I had never experienced before in my life. I said to myself: 'Yes, yes, I belong; these are my people. They may have a different color, religion or way of life, but they are my brothers and sisters. They love me, and I love them. Their smiles and tears are my smiles and tears; their prayers and prophecies are my prayers and prophecies, their anguish and hope are my anguish and hope. I am one with them.' In an instant, all differences seemed to melt away as snow in the sun. All my fears disappeared, and I felt surrounded by the welcoming arms of all humanity. Even though I was quite aware that some of the people with whom I held hands had spent years in prison, were addicted to drugs or alcohol, suffered from loneliness and depression and lived lives radically different from mine, to me they all looked like saints, radiant with God's love. They were, indeed, God's people, immensely loved and radically forgiven. The personal failings and shortcomings that had filled me with guilt and shame no longer seemed such a burden. All I felt was a deep sameness, a profound communion with all people and an exhilarating sense of brotherhood and sisterhood.

I am deeply convinced that it is this joy, the joy of being the same as others, of belonging to one human family that allows us to die well. I really do not know how I or anyone else can be prepared to die when our main concern is to count the trophies we have collected during our best years. The great gift hidden in our dying is the gift of unity with all people. However different we are, we all are born powerless, and we all die powerless, and the little differences we live in between dwindle in the light of this enormous truth. Often this human truth is presented as a reason to be sad. It is not seldom called a 'sobering truth.' But our great challenge is to discover this truth as a source of immense joy, setting us free to embrace our mortality with the awareness that we will make our passage to new life in solidarity with all the people of the earth.

A good death is a death in solidarity with others, and to prepare ourselves for a good death, we must develop or deepen this sense of solidarity. As long as we keep living toward our death as toward an event that separates us from people, our death cannot be much else than a sad and sorrowful event. But when we begin to grow in the awareness that our mortality, more than anything else, will lead us into solidarity with others, then our death can become a celebration of our unity with the human race. And so, instead of separating us from others, death can unite us with others; instead of being just sorrowful, it can give rise to new joy, and instead of being simply the end of life, it can become the beginning of something new.

At first this might sound absurd. How can our

dying and death create unity instead of separation? Isn't death the ultimate separation? It is, if we live by the norms of a competitive society always concerned with the question: 'Who is the strongest?' But when we claim our divine childhood and learn to trust that we belonged to God before we were born and will belong to God after we have died, then we come to experience that all people on this planet are, in fact, our brothers and sisters, making the journey through birth and death to new life with us. We are not alone; beyond all that separates us, we belong together. The mystery of life is that we discover this human togetherness, not when we are powerful and strong, but when we are vulnerable and weak.

The experiential knowledge that we will die like everyone else can fill us with a profound joy that makes it possible to face our death freely and fearlessly. It makes us not only say: 'It is good to live like everyone else,' but also, 'It is good to die like everyone else.' Some of us die earlier, some later; some of us die after a short life, others after a long life; some of us die after an illness, others suddenly and unexpectedly ... but all of us will die and participate in the same end. In light of this enormous human sameness, the many differences between the ways in which we live and die no longer have to separate us but can, to the contrary, deepen our sense of communion with one another. This communion with the whole human family, this profound sense of belonging to each other, takes the sting out of dying and points us far beyond the limits of our chronology. Somehow, we know that our bond with one another is stronger than death.

We touch here the core of Jesus's message. Jesus didn't come simply to point us away from this world by promising a new life after death. No, he came to make us aware that, as children of his God, we are all his brothers and sisters and brothers and sisters of each other and can, therefore, live our lives together without fear of death. Not only does he want us to participate in his divine childhood, he also wants us to enjoy fully the brotherhood and sisterhood that emerges from this shared childhood. He says to us: 'Just as the Father has loved me, so I have loved you' (John 15:9), and 'You must love one another, just as I have loved you' (John 13:34). The gospel writer, John, writing many years after Jesus's death, clearly shows the intimate connection between our being children of God and our being brothers and sisters of one another. He says: 'Let us love, then, because God loved us first. Anyone who says I love God and hates his brother or sister, is a liar, since whoever does not love the brother or sister that can be seen, cannot love God who cannot be seen. Indeed this is the commandment we have received, that whoever loves God, must also love his brother and sister' (John 4:19–21). It is the joy of this brotherhood and sisterhood that allows us to die well, because we no longer have to die alone but can die in intimate solidarity with all people on this planet. This solidarity offers hope. In Somalia and Ethiopia, children are dying. As their brothers and sisters, we must help them live, but we also must understand that we will die as they do. In Bosnia, Muslims, Croats and Serbs are dying. As their brothers and sisters we must do everything to prevent their killing each other, but we must also remain aware that we will die as they do. In Guatemala, Indians are dying. As their sisters and brothers we must work hard to stop their oppressors in their murderous work, but we must also face the fact that we will die as they do. In many countries, young and old people are dying of cancer and AIDS. As their brothers and sisters, we must care for them as well as we can and keep looking for cures, but we should never forget that we will die as they do. Countless men and women are dying through poverty and neglect. As their brothers and sisters we must offer them our resources and support. But we must remind ourselves continually that we will die as they do.

And so, in a mysterious way, the people dying all over the world because of starvation and oppression, illness and despair, violence and war become our teachers. In their immense pain and grief they ask us for solidarity, not only in life, but in death as well. Only when we are willing to let their dying help us to die well, will we be able to help them to live well because when we can face death with hope, we can live life with generosity.

We all die poor. When we come to our final hours, we have nothing any more that can help us to survive. No amount of money, power or influence can keep us from dying. This is true poverty. But Jesus says: 'Blessed are you who are poor; the Kingdom of God is yours' (Luke 6:20). There is a blessing hidden in the poverty of dying. It is the blessing that makes us into brothers and sisters in the same Kingdom. It is the blessing we receive from others who die. It is the blessing we give to others, when our time to die has come. It is the blessing that comes from the God whose life is everlasting. It is the blessing that reaches far beyond our birth and death. It is the blessing that carries us safely from eternity to eternity.

I would like to conclude this chapter with a story of a friend who was very ill. She had a great devotion to Mary, the mother of Jesus, and decided to make a pilgrimage to Lourdes in France asking for healing. When she left, I was afraid that she would be very disillusioned if no miracle were to happen. But on her return she said: 'Never did I see so many sick people. When I came face to face with that human suffering, I no longer wanted a miracle. I no longer wanted to be the exception. I experienced a deep desire to be one of them, to belong to these wounded people. Instead of praying for a cure, I prayed that I would have the grace to bear my illness in solidarity with them. And I trust that the Mother of Jesus will bring my prayer to her Son.'

I was deeply moved by this radical change in my friend's prayers. She, who had hoped to be different from all those who are ill, now wanted to be like them and live her pain as their sister in suffering.

This story reveals the healing power of the experience of human solidarity. This healing power, not only helps us to live our illness well, but our death too. Indeed, we can be healed from our fear of death, not by a miraculous event that prevents us from dying, but by the healing experience of being a brother and sister of all humans of the past, the present and the future, who share with us the fragility of our existence. In this experience we can taste the real joy of being human and have a foretaste of our communion with all people.

3

We Are Parents of Generations to Come

Marina, my sister-in-law, is only forty-eight years old. She is dying. Five years ago, her doctor told her that she had cancer. Ever since, her life has been a long, painful attempt to fight the illness and to survive the many medical interventions. With three major surgeries and much chemotherapy, medical experts tried to remove the cancer and to prolong Marina's life.

My brother Paul did everything possible to offer his wife hope that there was a chance to beat the enemy. But finally he realized, as others with him realized, that the battle was lost. As I write this, Marina is preparing herself for death.

During the last few years, I have often had the opportunity to talk to Marina about her illness and even about her death. Marina is a very strong, unsentimental woman. She likes to call a spade a spade and has no time for people who try to comfort or console her with 'white lies.' Although she cooperated fully with all the doctors and nurses who helped her to fight her cancer, she did not want anyone to make any decision of which she was not fully a part. Nor did she want any spiritual support that was based on religious convictions that she did not hold. She often questions my spiritual viewpoints and has strong opinions about life and death — her own as well as others'.

As the years went by and her illness got worse, Marina expressed herself more and more through painting and poetry. They started as a hobby, but gradually became her main way of living. The weaker she became physically, the stronger, more direct and less adorned became her artistic style. Her poems, especially, were the direct fruit of her struggle to befriend death. Marina had lived a very active and productive life. As a teacher and co-director of a language school, she had built a career for herself and shown great creativity in introducing new educational methods. But her illness had cruelly interrupted all of that and forced her to let go of the world she loved so much. Since her illness, her art became a new source of life for her. Often, when I was with her, she recited her poems by heart and asked me what I thought of them. Many of them were playful and often written with a humorous twist, but all of them expressed her increasing awareness that each day there was something more to let go of and that she was entering a time of many farewells.

As I saw how Marina prepared herself for her death, I gradually realized that she was making her own dying more and more a gift for others. Not only for my brother Paul, not only for her family and friends, but also for the nurses and doctors and the many circles of people with whom she spoke and shared her poems. Having taught all her life, she now taught through the way she prepared for her death. It struck me, suddenly, that her successes and accomplishments will probably be soon forgotten, but the fruits of her dying may well be long-lasting. Although her marriage remained childless and although she often had wondered during her life what her unique contribution to our society could be, the last five years might well prove to belong to the most fruitful years of her life. Not having had the joy of motherhood, she had become the parent of many through the way she lived towards her death. She showed me, in a whole new way, what it means to die for others. It means to become the parent of future generations.

Few words of Jesus have affected me personally so much as his words about his own approaching death. With great directness Jesus speaks to his closest friends about the end. Although he acknowledges the sorrow and sadness it will bring, he continues to announce his death as something good: something full of blessing, full of promise, full of hope. Shortly before his death he says: 'Now I am going to the one who sent me. No one of you asks, "Where are you going?" Yet you are sad at heart because I have told you this. Still, I am telling you the truth: it is for your own good that I am going, because unless I go, the Spirit will not come to you; but if I go, I will send him to you ... I shall have many things to say to you but they would be too much for you to bear now. However, when the Spirit of truth comes he will lead you to the complete truth, since he will not be speaking of his own accord, but will say only what he has been told; and he will reveal to you the things to come' (John 16: 4–7, 13).

At first, these words may sound strange and unfamiliar and even far away from our daily struggle with life and death, but after my conversation with Marina and with many other friends facing death, Jesus's words strike me in a new way and express the deepest significance of what they are experiencing. We may be inclined to look at the way Jesus prepared himself and his friends for his death as unique, far beyond our own 'normal' human way. But in fact, Jesus' way of dying offers us a very hopeful example. We, also, can say to our friends: 'It is for your own good that I am going ... because if I go I can send the Spirit to you and the Spirit will reveal to you the things to come.' Isn't this what Marina wants to say when she makes poems and paintings that will give new life to those who will mourn her death? Isn't 'sending the Spirit' the best expression for not leaving those you love alone but offering them a new bond, deeper than the bond that existed in life? Doesn't 'dying for others' mean dying so that others can continue strengthened by the Spirit of our love?

Perhaps you will protest saying 'Jesus, the only Son of the Father, did send his Holy Spirit to us — but we are not Jesus, and we have no Holy Spirit to send!' But when we listen deeply to Jesus's words, we come to realize that we are called to live like him, to die like him and to rise like him because the Spirit — the Divine Love, who makes Jesus one with his Father — has been given to us. And so, not only the death of Jesus, but our death too, is destined to be good for others. And further, not only the death of Jesus, but our death too, is meant to bear fruit in other people's lives. And finally, not only the death of Jesus, but our death, too, will bring the Spirit of God to those we leave behind. Yes, the great mystery is that all people who have lived with and in the Spirit of God, participate through their death, in the sending of the Spirit. Thus, God's Spirit of love continues to be sent to us and reveals how Jesus' death continues to bear fruit through all whose death is like his death, a death for others.

In this way, dying becomes the way to an everlasting fruitfulness. We touch here the most hope-giving aspect of our death. Our death may be the end of our success, our productivity, our fame or our importance among people, but it is not the end of our fruitfulness. The opposite is true; the fruitfulness of our lives shows itself in its fullness only after we have died. We ourselves seldom see or experience our fruitfulness. Often we remain too pre-occupied with our accomplishments and have no eye for the fruitfulness of what we live. But the beauty of life is that it bears fruit long after life itself has come to an end. Jesus says: 'In all truth I tell you, unless a wheat grain falls into the earth and dies, it remains only a single grain; but if it dies, it yields a rich harvest' (John 12:24).

This is the mystery of Jesus' death and of the deaths of all who lived in his Spirit. Their lives yield fruit far beyond the limits of their short and often very localized existence. Years after my mother's death she continues to bear fruit in my life. I am deeply aware that many of my major decisions, since her death, were guided by the Spirit of Jesus that she continues to send me.

Jesus lived less than forty years; he didn't travel outside his own country; the people who knew him during his life scarcely understood him; and when he died, only a very few of his followers remained faithful. In every respect his life was a failure. Success had left him, popularity had dwindled, and all his power was gone. Still, few lives have been so fruitful; few lives have affected people's thinking and feeling so deeply; few lives have so profoundly shaped future cultures, and few lives have influenced so radically the patterns of human relationships. Jesus himself refers constantly to the fruitfulness of his life that will only become manifest after his death. Often, he stresses that his disciples do not comprehend what he is saying or doing but that one day they will understand. When he washes Peter's feet he says: 'At the moment you do not know what I am doing, but later you will understand' (John 13:7). And when he speaks about his return to the Father he says again: 'I have said these things to you while still with you, but ... the holy Spirit whom the Father will send in my name, will teach you everything and remind you of all that I have said to you' (John 14:25–6). The full meaning of Jesus's life was only revealed after his death. Isn't this also true of many of the great men and women in history? Often, the full meaning of their lives becomes clear long after they have died. Some of them were barely known during their lives, and some were known for completely different things than the things they are remembered for today. Some of them were very successful and famous, others suffered from endless failures and rejections. But all truly great men and women who have shaped our ways of thinking and acting, have borne fruit that they themselves couldn't see or even predict.

There are many illustrations of this; I would like to present here the example of Brother Lawrence.

This simple lay brother lived as a cook and shoemaker in a French Carmelite house of studies from 1614 to 1691. After his death, his letters and reflections about 'walking in the presence of God' were made public, and even today they continue to affect the spiritual life of many people. His life was quite unspectacular but very, very fruitful. Lawrence himself, however, never thought much about influencing other people's lives. His only wish was to do all that he did — especially his kitchen work — in the presence of God!

All of this is to show that the real question before our death is not: 'How much can I still accomplish, or how much influence can I still exert?' but: 'How can I so live that I can continue to be fruitful when I am no longer here among my family and friends?' That question shifts our attention from doing to being. Our doing brings success, but our being bears fruit. The great paradox of our lives is that while we are often very concerned about what we do, or still can do, we are most likely to be remembered for who we were. If it was the Spirit that guided our lives — the Spirit of love, joy, peace, gentleness, forgiveness, courage, perseverance, hope and faith — that Spirit that will not die but continue to grow from generation to generation.

Pondering Marina's death and my own, I realize the great challenge of life. While the society in which I live, keeps asking for the tangible results of my life, I must gradually learn to trust that the results of my life, may or may not prove to be significant, but that what really counts are the fruits that it bears. As I grow older and weaker, I will be able to do less and less. Both my body and my mind will become weaker. My eyes will move closer to the book I want to read and my ears closer to the neighbor I am trying to understand. My failing memory will lead me to repeat my jokes more often, and my decreasing ability to reflect critically will turn me into a less interesting conversationalist. Nonetheless, I trust that in my weakness God's Spirit will manifest itself and that from my deteriorating body and mind, God's Spirit will move where it wants and bear fruit.

And so my death will indeed be a rebirth. Something new will come to be, something about which I cannot say or think much. It lies beyond my own chronology. It is something that will last and carry on from generation to generation. In this way, I become a new parent, a parent of the future.

Before concluding this chapter, I want to speak about my friends with AIDS. I think of them every day. Some I know personally, some I know because they are friends of friends, and many I know because of what is written by them or about them. From the outset of this horrendous epidemic, I have felt very close to the many young men and women who live with AIDS. They all know that they cannot live long and that they will die difficult and often painful deaths. I want so much to help them, be with them, console and comfort them. I am overwhelmed by the tragedy that, in their desperate desire to be embraced and cared for, many have found illness and death instead. I cry out to heaven saying: 'Why, O God, does the human search for communion and intimacy lead to separation and anguish? Why are so many young people who simply want to be loved, languishing in hospitals and lonely rooms? Why are love and death so close to each other?' Maybe the 'why?' is not what is important. Important are the men and women with their beautiful names and beautiful faces who wonder why they didn't find the love they yearned for. I feel very close to them because their pain is not far from mine. I, too, want to love and be loved. I, too, have to die. I, too, know that mysterious connection between my heart's yearning for love and my heart's anguish. In my heart I want to embrace and hold all these people who are dying, hungry for love.

Do I have anything to say to them? Recently I read Paul Monette's deeply moving book *Borrowed Time*. There he describes in pain-filled detail his battle against the AIDS of his friend George Horowitz. The whole book is like one battle cry: 'We will beat the enemy. We will not let this evil force destroy our lives.' It is a heroic battle in which every means of survival is tried. But it is a lost battle. George dies, and Paul remains alone. Is death finally stronger than love? Are we, finally, all losers? Is all our struggle to survive, in the end, a silly struggle, as silly as the struggle of a fox to gnaw its way out of a leg trap?

Many must feel that way. Only their deep, human self-respect in the face of the unbeatable power of death makes them put up an honest fight. I have a deep admiration for the way Paul and George fought their grim battle. But after a life of reflection on the death of Jesus and many of his followers, I want to believe that beyond the fatal battle for survival there is a hopeful battle for life. I do want to believe — indeed, I do believe — that, ultimately, love is stronger than death. I have no argument to present. I have only the story of Jesus and the stories of those who trust in the life-giving truth of his life and his word. These stories show me a new way of living and a new way of dying, and I have a deep desire to show that way to others.

When I visited Rick in Bethany House, the Catholic Workers house for people with AIDS, in Oakland, California, I wanted to say something to him that Paul hadn't been able to say to George. In Paul's experience, the churches had nothing significant to say to people with AIDS. To the contrary, he could only think of them as hypocritical, oppressive and rejecting. He found more comfort in Greek mythology than in the Christian story. But when I held Rick's hand and looked into his fear-filled eyes, I felt deeply that the short time he had still to live could be more than a brave, but losing battle for survival. I wanted him to know and believe that the meaning of the time left lay, not in what he could still do, but in the fruits he could bear when there was nothing left to do. When we were together, Rick said: 'My friends shall have a future. I have only death to wait for.' I didn't know what to say, and I knew that a lot of words wouldn't do him much good. Instead, I took his hand in mine and laid my other hand on his forehead; I looked into his tearful eyes and said: 'Rick don't be afraid, don't be afraid, God is very close to you, much closer than I am. Please trust that the time ahead of you will be the most important time of your life, not just for you, but for all of us whom you love and who love you.' As I said these words, I felt his body relax, and a smile came through his tears. He said 'Thank you, thank you.' Then he reached out his arms and pulled me very close to him whispering in my ear: 'I want to believe you, I really do, but it is so hard.'

As I think of Rick and the many young people who are dying like him, everything in me rises up in protest. But I know that it is a temptation to think of them as people who are fighting a losing battle. With all the faith I can muster, I believe that their deaths will be fruitful and that they are indeed called to be the parents of the generations to come.

The Choice to Die Well

To befriend death, we have to claim that we are children of God, sisters and brothers of all people and parents of the generations yet to come. In so doing, we liberate our death from its absurdity and make it into the gateway to new life.

In our society, in which childhood is only something to grow away from, in which brotherhood and sisterhood among people are constantly mocked by wars and ethnic conflicts, and in which the greatest emphasis is on 'making it' in the few years we have, it seems hardly possible to think of death as a gateway to anything!

Still, Jesus has opened this way for us. When we choose his way to live and die, we will be able to face our death with the mocking question of the apostle Paul: 'Death where is your victory? Death, where is your sting?' (1 Cor. 15:55). But this is a choice, a very hard choice. The powers of darkness that surround us are so strong that we are easily tempted to let our fear of death rule our thoughts, words and actions. Nevertheless we can choose to befriend our death as Jesus did. We can choose to live as God's beloved children in solidarity with all people, trusting in our ultimate fruitfulness.

61

And in so doing, we can also become people who care for others. As men and women who have faced our mortality, we can help our brothers and sisters to dispel the darkness of death and guide them toward the light of God's grace. So, let us turn now to the subject of care.

PART II
CARING WELL

At the Heart of Being Human

Befriending our death is a life-long spiritual task, but a task that, in all its different nuances, deeply affects our relationships with our fellow human beings. Every step we take toward a deeper self-understanding is also a step that brings us closer to those with whom we share our lives. As we learn, over time, to live the truth that death no longer has a 'sting,' we discover within ourselves the gift to guide others to the discovery of the same truth. It's not a question of 'first' and 'later.' Befriending our own death and helping others to befriend theirs are inseparable. They belong together. In the realm of the Spirit of God, living and caring are one. Our society keeps suggesting that caring is something quite separate from living and belongs primarily to professionals who have received special training.

Although training is important, and although certain people need special preparation to practice their profession with competence, ... to care is the privilege of every person and is at the heart of being human.

When we go back to the original meaning of the word profession, and realize that it refers, first of all, to professing one's own deepest conviction, then the essential spiritual unity between living and caring becomes clear.

In the following three chapters I would like to reflect on caring for the dying. I want, first of all, to look at caring for the dying as helping our fellow human beings in befriending their own deaths. In these reflections I hope to make it clear that, to the degree that we ourselves have befriended our own death, we can become truly caring people. Paralleling the first three chapters of this book, I will look at care as helping others to claim for themselves the spiritual truth that they are — as we are — children of God, brothers and sisters of each other and parents of the generations to come.

4

You Are a Child of God

Maurice Gould, who died ten days before I began writing this book, was one of the first people I met at Daybreak. He was a member of the 'Green House,' the house where I spent my first week. Moe was born with Down's Syndrome. For many years he lived with his parents and sister, who cared for him lovingly. When he was in his early forties he came to Daybreak. Two years ago, Maurice began to show signs of Alzheimer's disease. From then until his death, the community tried to care for him in the special way that Alzheimer patients require. The doctors told us that Moe would not be able to live long and that we had to prepare him, as well as ourselves, for his death.

For those who were close to Moe — his family, his friends and those who lived with him in the Green House — caring for him became a great challenge, a challenge at once painful and joyful.

As Moe gradually lost his memory, his ability to recognize people, his sense of orientation and his ability to feed himself, he became more and more anxious and could no longer be his old good-humored self. It was very hard to see him slip away into a state of complete dependency, needing more help than we could offer him. Finally, he was brought to the nearby hospital, where a very competent staff, together with the members of the Green House, cared for him during the last months of his life.

One of the things I remember most about Moe, were his generous hugs. Often, he walked up to me with both hands stretched out and always ready for a big embrace. As he held me he would whisper in my ear: 'Amazing Grace,' hoping that I would sing his favorite song with him. I also remember his love for dancing, his love of food and his love for making people laugh with his imitations. When he imitated me, he put his glasses upside down on his nose and made wild gestures!

Now as I sit in Freiburg, far away from my community, and think of Moe, I realize more than ever that Moe was, and became ever more, a child of God. Being allowed to be so close to his 'second childhood' enabled his friends to care for him with great patience and lavish generosity.

Moe's illnesses — Down's Syndrome and Alzheimer's disease — showed, in a dramatic way, the journey we all have to make somewhere, some-how. But at the end of that journey, what do we finally see? Do we see a person who has lost all his human abilities and become a burden for everyone, or do we see a person who has become ever more a child of God, a pure instrument of grace? I cannot help but think about the countless times Moe looked me in the eyes and said again: 'Amazing Grace.' I was not always ready to sing the old song again, and often I said: 'Next time Moe, not now,' but now that Moe is gone, I keep hearing his so persistent words, 'Amazing Grace, Amazing Grace,' as God's way of announcing to me the mystery of Moe's life, and that of all people.

In Daybreak, many of us cannot do what most people can. Some of us cannot walk, some cannot speak, some cannot feed themselves, some cannot read, some cannot count, some cannot dress themselves, and a few can do none of these things. No one is waiting for a cure. We only know that things will get harder as we get older and that the difference between people with a handicap and people without a handicap will become ever smaller. What are we ultimately growing toward? Are we simply becoming less and less capable people, returning our bodies to the dust from which they came, or are we growing into living reminders of that 'Amazing Grace' that Moe always wanted to sing about?

We must choose between these two radically different viewpoints. The choice to see our own and other people's decreasing abilities as gateways for God's increasing grace is a choice of faith. It is a choice based on the conviction that on the cross of Jesus we do see, not only failure, but victory as well, not only destruction, but new life as well, not only nakedness, but glory as well. When John, the beloved disciple, looked up to Jesus and saw blood and water flowing from his pierced side, he saw something other than a clear proof that it was over. He saw the fulfillment of the prophecy, 'they will look up to the one whom they have pierced,' (Zech. 12:10) a glimpse of God's victory over death, and a sign of God's amazing grace. He writes: 'This is evidence of the one who saw it — true evidence, and he knows that what he says is true — and he gives it so that you may believe as well' (John 19:35).

That's the choice of faith. It is the choice we make when we dare to say that Moe, whose body and mind were completely depleted by Alzheimer's disease, is bringing to us, through his dying and death, an amazing Grace! It's the choice we make when we care for dying people with all the tenderness and gentleness that God's beloved children deserve. It's the choice that allows us to see the face of Jesus in the poor, the addicted and those who live with AIDS and cancer. It's the choice of the human heart that has been touched by the Spirit of Jesus and is able to recognize that Spirit wherever there are people dying.

When, recently, I was visited by the leaders of several Christian institutions responsible for the supervision of homes for people with mental disabilities, they told me that, in our free-market economy, human care is spoken of in terms of supply and demand. In this context, the suffering person becomes the buyer of care, and the care professional becomes the merchant of care. When I heard this, I wondered how this language and the vision that underlies it, could prevent the human person from becoming nothing but a commodity in the competitive world of high finance. Here, a choice has been made for a vision that no longer has a language that encourages the celebration of the dying and death of people like Maurice Gould. Amazing Grace has been replaced by many, not so amazing, business considerations.

Care, as I speak of it here, is the loving attention given to another person, not because they need it to stay alive, not because they or their insurance companies are paying for it, not because they provide jobs, not because the law does not permit us to hasten their death, and not because they can be used for medical research, but ... because they are children of God as we are.

To care for others as they become weaker and closer to death, is to allow them to fulfill their deepest vocation, that of becoming ever more fully what they already are: daughters and sons of God. It is to help them to claim, especially in their dying hours, their divine childhood and to let the Spirit of God cry out from their hearts, 'Abba, Father' (Gal. 4: 6). To care for the dying is to keep saying: 'You are the beloved daughter of God, you are the beloved son of God.'

How do we say this? The ways are countless. There are words, prayers and blessings; there is the gentle touch and the holding of hands; there is cleaning and feeding, and listening and just being there. Some of these forms of care may be helpful, some not. But all of them are ways of expressing our faith, that those we care for are precious in God's eyes. Through our caring presence we want to keep announcing that sacred truth. Dying is not a sweet sentimental event. It is a great struggle: the struggle to surrender our lives completely. But this surrender is not an obvious human response. To the contrary: we want to cling to whatever is left, and it is for this reason that there is so much anguish in dying people. As Jesus, they, too, often experience their total powerlessness, as being rejected and abandoned. Often the agonizing cry: 'My God, my God why have you abandoned me?' (Matthew 27: 46), makes it nearly impossible to say: 'Father into your hands I commend my Spirit' (Luke 23: 46).

Moe wasn't spared this struggle. As the Alzheimer's disease took away his already limited abilities to direct his own life, a great anguish grew within him. He often cried out in agony, and he experienced an ever-growing fear of being left alone. Often, during the night, he wanted to get up and go to work. Two of the last words he could still say were: 'Call me . . . call me . . . call me.' Moe's fear is no different from my own. It is the fear of being rejected or left alone; of being found a burden, a nuisance or a 'pain in the neck'; of being laughed at, or considered useless; . . . it is the deep fear of not belonging, of excommunication, of final abandonment. The more intimately I come to know people with mental handicaps, the more I am convinced that their deepest suffering is not their inability to read, study, speak or walk, but their deep fear of being rejected as a burden, and in this respect they do not differ from me. My greatest suffering is located precisely in that moment when I lose touch with my own belovedness and can only think of myself as a useless, unwanted presence.

Caring for others is, first of all, helping them to overcome that enormous temptation of self-rejection. Whether we are rich or poor, famous or unknown, handicapped or not, we all share the fear of being left alone and abandoned. And this fear is always hidden under the surface of our self-composure. It is rooted much more deeply than is the possibility of not being liked or loved by people. It's deepest root lies in the possibility of not being loved at all, of not belonging to anything that lasts,

of being swallowed up by a dark nothingness, yes
. . . of being abandoned by God.

Caring, therefore, is being present to people as
they fight this ultimate battle, a battle that
becomes ever more real and intense as death
approaches. Dying and death always call forth, with
renewed power, the fear that we are unloved and
will finally be reduced to useless ashes. To care is
to stand by a dying person and to be a living
reminder that that person is, indeed, the beloved
child of God.

Mary's standing under the cross is the most
moving expression of that care. Her son is dying in
agony. She is there: not speaking, not pleading,
not crying. She is there reminding her son by her
silent presence that, while she cannot keep him for
herself, his true sonship belongs to the Father,
who will never leave him alone. She helps him recall
his own words: 'the time will come . . . when you will
leave me alone. And yet I am not alone, because
the Father is with me' (John 16:32). She
encourages him to move beyond his experience of
abandonment and to surrender himself into the
embrace of his Father. She is there to strengthen
his faith that, even in the midst of darkness, where
he can feel nothing but loss and rejection, he
remains the beloved Son of God, who will not ever
leave him alone. It is this motherly care that finally
allows Jesus to win the battle against the demonic
powers of rejection, to ward off the temptation of

abandonment and to surrender his whole being to God with the words: 'Father into your hands I commend my Spirit' (Luke 23: 46).

Can we care as Mary did? I don't believe we can . . . on our own. Even Mary was not alone. John, the beloved disciple, was there with her beneath the cross. Reminding people in their agony of their divine childhood, is not something we can do on our own. The powers of darkness are strong, and we can easily be pulled into the darkness ourselves and drawn into enormous self-doubts. Standing by a person who is dying is participating in the immense struggle of faith. It's a struggle no person should want to take on alone. Before we realize it, the anguish of our dying friend becomes ours, and so we become the victim of the same powers our friend is struggling with. We become overwhelmed by feelings of helplessness, powerlessness, self-doubt and even feelings of guilt, linked to our often unacknowledged wish that it all will end soon.

No, we shouldn't try to care by ourselves. Care is not an endurance test. We should, whenever possible, care together with others. It is the community of care that reminds the dying person of his/her belovedness. It is Mary *and* John, it is Lori *and* Carl, Loretta *and* David, Carol *and* Peter, Janice *and* Cheryl, Geoff *and* Carrie, Lorenzo and many others, who together can stand at the foot of the cross and say: 'You are the beloved child of

God, now as always.' This circle of love, surrounding our dying friends has the power to expel the demons of self-rejection and abandonment and bring light in the midst of the darkness. I saw it happening around Moe; I see it happening in the AIDS community and in the networks of support for cancer patients. Together, as a body of love, as a community that cares, we can come very close to the dying and discover there new hope, new life and a new strength to live. There can be smiles and little stories; there can be new encounters and new knowledge about ways to help; there can be beautiful moments of silence and prayer; there can be the gift of just being together, waiting patiently for death to come. Together we can create that place where our dying friends can feel safe and can gradually let go and make the passage with the knowledge of being loved.

Caring together is the basis of community life. We don't come together simply to console each other or even to support each other. Important as that may be, long-term community life is directed in other ways. Together we want to reach out to others. Together we want to look at those who need our care. Together we want to carry our suffering brothers and sisters to the place of rest, healing and safety.

I have always been impressed with the thought that people are only ready to commit themselves to each other when they no longer focus on each other but focus together on the larger world beyond them. Falling in love makes us look at each other with admiration and tenderness. Committing ourselves to one another in love makes us look together towards those who need our care: the child, the stranger, the poor and the dying. That commitment lies at the heart of every community.

When I reflect on my own community, the L'Arche Daybreak community in Toronto, I realize increasingly that what keeps us faithful to each other is our common commitment to care for people with mental disabilities. We are called to care together. No one in our community would be able to care singlehandedly for any one of our handicapped members. Not only would it be physically impossible, but it would quickly lead to emotional and mental exhaustion as well. Together, however, we can create a caring space that is good not only for those who receive care, but also for those who give it. It is precisely in this space that the boundaries between receiving and giving vanish and true community can start to exist. It is essential to the weakest members of our community that those who care for them do so together. They say to us: 'For me to live, you must love, not just me, but each other too.'

When I reflect on the ups and downs of community life through the ages, I can easily see how the 'ups' are closely connected to the vibrancy of caring together and the 'downs' with the absorption in internal matters. Even the most contemplative, seemingly hidden, community could stay alive and well only when their life remained a life for others. Even a life completely dedicated to prayer and meditation always needs to maintain a quality of caring together for others.

The mystery of this caring together is that it not only asks for community, but also creates it.

Those who cared for Moe realized, after his death, that he had brought them closer than they were before. Just as the dying Jesus brought Mary and John closer to each other by giving them to each other as mother and son, so too did Moe bring his friends closer to each other as sons and daughters of the same God; all true care for the dying person, brings a new awareness of the bonds that create a community of love.

Before concluding this chapter, I would like to tell a story about 'the Flying Rodleighs.' They are trapeze artists who perform in the German circus Simoneit-Barum. When the circus came to Freiburg two years ago, my friends Franz and Reny invited me and my father to see the show. I will never forget how enraptured I became when I first saw the Rodleighs move through the air, flying and catching, as elegant dancers. The next day I returned to the circus to see them again and introduced myself to them as one of their great fans. They invited me to attend their practice sessions, gave me free tickets, asked me to dinner and suggested I travel with them for a week in the near future. I did ... and we became good friends.

One day I was sitting with Rodleigh, the leader of the troupe, in his caravan, talking about flying. He said: 'As a flyer I must have complete trust in my catcher. You and the public might think that I am the great star of the trapeze, but the real star is Joe, my catcher. He has to be there for me with split-second precision and grab me out of the air as I come to him in the long jump!' 'How does it work?' I asked. 'Well,' Rodleigh said, 'the secret is that the flyer does nothing and the catcher everything! When I fly to Joe, I have simply to stretch out my arms and hands waiting for him to catch me and pull me safely over the apron behind the catchbar.'

'You do nothing!' I said quite surprised. 'Nothing,' Rodleigh repeated. 'The worst thing the flyer can do is to try to catch the catcher. I am not supposed to catch Joe. It's Joe's task to catch me. If I grabbed Joe's wrists, I might break them, or he might break mine and that would be the end for both of us! A flyer has to fly and a catcher has to catch, and the flyer has to trust, with outstretched arms, that his catcher will be there for him!'

When Rodleigh said this with so much conviction, the words of Jesus flashed through my mind: 'Father into your hands I commend my Spirit' (Luke 23:46). Dying is trusting in the Catcher! Caring for the dying is saying: 'Don't be afraid, remember you are the Beloved Son of God. He will

be there when you make your long jump, ... don't
try to grab him, he will grab you, ... just stretch out
your arms and hands and trust, trust, trust.'

5

You Are Brothers and Sisters of Each Other

One day, Sally, a good friend of mine, said: 'It has been five years since my husband Bob died, and I would like to visit his grave with my children. Would you be willing to come with us?' When I said: 'Of course, I would love to come with you,' she told me what had happened. Bob had died very unexpectedly from heart failure, and Sally suddenly was faced with the hard task of helping her children Mitchell and Lindsay, who were four and five at the time, to respond to their father's death. She felt that it would be too hard for the children to see their father being put into the ground and covered with sand. 'They are much too young to understand,' Sally thought. But as the years went by, the cemetery had become a fearful place for Sally, Lindsay and Mitchell.

Intuitively, Sally felt that something was not right.

Thus she invited me to go with her and the children to Bob's grave. For Lindsay it was still a little too scary, so only Mitchell came along.

It was a beautiful, sunny day. We soon found Bob's grave, a simple stone engraved with the words: 'A kind and gentle man.' We sat on the grass around the stone, and Sally and Mitchell told stories about Bob. Mitchell remembered how his dad played ball with him. When his memory became hazy, Sally filled in the details. And I? I just asked questions. As we were beginning to feel more at ease I said: 'Wouldn't it be nice to have a picnic here? Maybe one day we all can come back, bring food and drinks with us and celebrate Bob's life . . . right here at his grave. We could eat together in his memory!' At first Sally and Mitchell were a little puzzled with the idea, but then Mitchell said: 'Yes, why not, and then I am sure Lindsay will come too.'

When Sally and Mitchell came home they told Lindsay that it hadn't been scary at all but quite okay. A few days later, Lindsay asked Sally to take her to the grave. They went and talked together about Bob. Gradually, Bob became less a stranger and more like a new friend, and having a picnic on his grave became something to look forward to. After all, Jesus too had asked his friends to remember him with a meal!

This story shows how easily we distance ourselves from those who have died and treat them as fearful strangers who remind us of things we don't want to be reminded of ... especially our own mortality. But this story also shows how easily we can bring those who have died back into the circle of the living and make them gentle friends who can help us to face our own death.

How often do we see someone die? How often do we see a dead person? How often do we throw sand on top of a coffin that has been lowered into the grave? How often do we go to the cemetery and stand, kneel or sit in front of the place where our spouse, our parents, our brothers, sisters, aunts, uncles or friends have been buried? Are we still in touch with those who have died, or are we living our lives as if those who lived before us had never really existed?

In Geysteren, the little village in the southern part of Holland where my father lives, the dead are still part of the daily life of the people. The cemetery, close to the village square, is a beautifully-kept garden. The gate is freshly painted, the hedges well-trimmed, the walkways raked clean and each grave well cared for. Many of the memorial crosses or stones are decorated with fresh flowers or evergreen plants. The cemetery feels like a place where visitors are welcome and where it is good to spend time. The villagers love their cemetery. They go there often to pray and to be with their family or friends who have left them. During each service in the village church 'those who rest in our cemetery' are mentioned and included in the prayers of the community.

Whenever I visit my father in Geysteren, I go to that little cemetery. Close to the entrance, on the left side, is my mother's grave, marked with a simple brown wooden cross on which her name and the dates of her birth and death are painted in white. In front of the cross, evergreen plants outline the place where her body is laid to rest, and newly planted violets cover the center. When I stand before that simple grave, look at the cross and hear the wind play with the leaves of the tall poplars surrounding the cemetery, I know that I am not alone. She is there and speaks to me. There is no apparition, no mysterious voice, but there is the simple inner knowledge that she who died more than fourteen years ago is still with me. Embraced by the solitude of the beautiful cemetery, I hear her say that I must be faithful to my own journey and not be afraid to join her some day in death.

As I stand there in front of my mother's grave, the circles of the dead surrounding me become ever wider. I am surrounded, not only by the villagers who lie buried there, but also by family members and friends. Even wider is the circle of all those whose actions and words have shaped my life and thoughts. And beyond, there are the many circles of the countless men and women whose names I do not know but who have, in their own unique way, made the journey that I am making and shared in the pains and joys of being human.

The poplars of the little cemetery in Geysteren sing their songs for all these people buried wide and far. Some were buried with the same gentleness as my mother was, some were simply put away and forgotten, and many were dumped into large mass graves of which few know the location and where no one ever comes to pray. For all of them, the poplars sing, and standing there I feel grateful for being human, as all these people were, and for being called to die, as they did.

What a gift it is to know deeply that we are brothers and sisters in the one human family and that, different as our cultures, languages, religions, lifestyles or work may be, we are all mortal beings called to surrender our lives into the hands of a loving God. What a gift it is to feel connected with the many who have died and to discover the joy and peace that flows from that connectedness. As I experience that gift, I know in a new way what it means to care for the dying. It means to connect them with the many who are dying or have died and to let them discover the intimate bonds that reach far beyond the boundaries of our short lives.

To go with Sally and Mitchell to Bob's grave and then to stand silently in the Geysteren cemetery in front of the place where my mother is buried, strengthens me in the conviction that all who are dying should know about the deep communion that exists between all men and women on this planet. We human beings belong together, whether we live now or long ago, whether we live close by or far away, whether we have biological ties or not. We are brothers and sisters, and our dying is truly a dying in communion with each other.

But when we look at the world around us, the question arises: do we really live as brothers and sisters? Every day, the newspapers and television remind us that human beings are fighting each other, torturing each other, killing each other. All over the world people are the victims of persecution, war and starvation. All over the world there is hatred, violence and abuse. For a while, we lived with the illusion that the period of concentration camps was far behind us, and that a holocaust, such as that which occurred during the Second World War, would no longer be humanly possible. But what is happening today shows how very little we have really learned. The true sin of humanity is that men and women created to be each other's brothers and sisters, become over and over again each other's enemies, willing to destroy each other's lives.

God sent Jesus to restore the true human order. He is called the Redeemer. He came to redeem us from our sins and to remind us of the truth that we are sons and daughters of God, brothers and sisters of one another.

How did Jesus redeem us from our sins? By becoming one of us: being born as we are born, living as we live, suffering as we suffer and dying as we die. Indeed, by becoming our brother: God-with-us. When the angel of God came to Nazareth and spoke to Joseph in a dream, he said: 'Joseph, son of David, do not be afraid to take Mary home as your wife because she has conceived what is in her by the Holy Spirit. She will give birth to a son and you must name him Jesus, because he is the one who is to save his people from their sins.' The evangelist Matthew, who wrote this, added: 'Now all this took place to fulfill what the Lord had spoken through the prophet: 'Look! the virgin is with child and will give birth to a son whom they will call Immanuel,' a name which means "God-with-us"' (Matt. 1:20–24).

God became 'God-with-us,' our brother, so that we might claim for ourselves our brotherhood and sisterhood with all people. That is the story of Jesus, the story of our redemption. The heart of that story is that, in and through Jesus, God not only wanted to share our life, but our death as well. Jesus' death is the most radical expression of God's desire to be God-with-us.' There is nothing that makes all human beings so similar to each other as their mortality. It is our common mortality that shows the illusion of our differences, the falseness of the many divisions among us and the sins of our mutual enmities. By dying with and for us, Jesus wants to dispel our illusions, heal our divisions and forgive our sins so that we can

rediscover that we are each other's brothers and
sisters. By becoming our brother, Jesus wants us
to become again brothers and sisters for one
another. In nothing, but sin, does he want to differ
from us. That is why he died for us. As one who was
as mortal as we are, Jesus calls us to stop living in
fear of each other and to start loving one another.
And this is more than his wish. It is his commandment because it belongs to the essence of our
being human. He says: 'This is my commandment,
love one another as I have loved you. No one can
have greater love than to lay down his life for his
friends. You are my friends, if you do what I
command you, I shall no longer call you servants,
because a servant does not know his master's
business; I call you friends because I have made
known to you everything that I have learnt from my
Father... My command to you is to love one
another' (John 15: 12–17).

This great mystery of God becoming God-with-
us, has very radical implications for the way we care
for the dying. When God wants to die with and for
us, we too have to die with and for each other.
Tragically, however, we think about our death, first
of all, as an event that separates us from others.
It is departing. It is leaving others behind. It
is the ending of precious relationships. It is
the beginning of loneliness. Indeed, for us, death
is primarily a separation and, even worse, an irre-
versible separation.

But Jesus died for us so that our death no longer has to be just separation. His death opened the possibility for us to make our own death a way to union and communion. That's the radical turn that our faith allows us to make. But making that turn does not happen spontaneously. It requires care.

To care for the dying means to make them live their dying as a way to gather around them, not only those who come to visit, not only family and friends, but all of humanity, the living as well as the dead. When we say that it is not good for a human being to die alone, we touch a very deep mystery. It is the mystery that precisely in our death we need to be, more than ever, in communion with others. The passage of our life is the passage that, more than any other passage, needs to be made with others.

There is something so obvious about this that no one would ever question the importance of being with someone at the moment of death. One of our worst fears about dying is to have to die without anyone at our side. We want someone to hold our hand, someone to touch us and speak gently to us, someone to pray with us. And that's what we want to do for others.

But there is more, much more, that is less obvious. To care, also means gently to encourage our dying friend to die with and for others. Somehow, we who care need to have the courage to bring together around our dying friends the saints and sinners of all times: the starving children, the tortured prisoners, the homeless, the wanderers, the AIDS-afflicted and the thousands, yes millions, of people who have died or are now dying. At first this might seem harsh, even cruel, but the opposite is true. It lifts our dying friends out of their isolation and makes them part of the most human of all human events. When those who are dying begin to realize that what they are experiencing is something that, although very painful, unites them with the worldwide and centuries-old family of humanity, they may be able to let go and, bit by bit, let that human family carry them through the gate of death.

This is the reason why, through the course of Christian history, dying people have been encouraged to look at the cross. On the famous sixteenth century 'Isenheimer Altar' in Colmar, France, Christ is portrayed hanging on the cross in unspeakable agony. His whole body is covered with sores caused by the black plague. But when those who were dying of the plague looked up at that suffering Christ, they saw there, not only Jesus, who died with and for them long ago, but also all their dying brothers and sisters. There they found consolation. They realized that, as Christ had died for them, they too could die for their brothers and sisters and so make their dying an act of human solidarity. Recently, in San Francisco, I saw a cross on which Jesus was dying of AIDS. There too, all men, women and children of the world with AIDS were portrayed, not to frighten, but to offer hope. This AIDS cross is a cross for the dying people of our century to look up to and find hope.

Caring, therefore, is something very different from protecting dying people from seeing the larger picture. To the contrary, it is helping them to grow in the awareness that their individual, painful condition is embedded in the basic condition of human mortality and, as such, can be lived in communion with others.

This care can be seen today in the many AIDS communities. In different cities in North America, young people are supporting each other to live their illness in solidarity with each other and with others who are dying. They may seldom think or talk about this solidarity as an expression of God's solidarity with us, but whether they think or talk in this way or not, they do help each other to die in the same spirit in which Jesus died, the spirit of communion with the larger human family.

Is there anything 'practical' to say about care for the dying in this perspective? Maybe only that dying people can face the reality of life much better than care givers often realize. We have a tendency to keep the 'bad news' of our world hidden from those who are dying. We want to offer them a quiet, undisturbed and 'peaceful' end. To accomplish that, we are inclined to avoid telling them about other people who are sick or dying, to avoid speaking with them about the victims of war and starvation in other places of the world. We want to keep them separated from the terrible realities of life. But do we offer them a service in doing so? Or do we prevent them from living their illness in solidarity with their fellow human beings and making their death a death with and for others?

Every illness, and especially a terminal illness, tends to narrow people's vision because they become quickly preoccupied with their own medical ups and downs and the daily events connected with their health. And the often repeated question: 'How are you doing?' encourages people to tell and retell their own story, often against their own desire.

Still, I think, there are many people who desire to remain part of the larger world and who would gladly hear and speak about things going on outside their home or hospital. I remember vividly how grateful I was during my own illness for visitors who didn't ask or speak about me, but focused my attention on something larger than myself.

In fact, I felt grateful not to be separated from the world. I felt encouraged and strengthened by the assumption of my friends that my illness did not prevent me from being truly interested in the struggle, of other people. Being connected and constantly reconnected with the larger suffering of my brothers and sisters in the human family did not paralyze me. To the contrary, it had a healing effect. This healing came from not being infan-tilized but treated as a mature adult able to live his pain together with others.

I am not suggesting that we care for dying people simply by telling them about all the misery in the world! That would be unwise and unhelpful. I am not speaking here about causing our dying friends to worry about the suffering of others. I am only saying that, when we ourselves have befriended our own mortality, we will have no need to isolate our dying friends and will intuitively know how to maintain their communion with the larger, suffer-ing human family. When we who care are not afraid to die, we will be better able to prepare the dying for death and, instead of separating them from others, will deepen their communion with them.

I would like to conclude this chapter, as I did the other chapters, with a story.

A few years ago, the IMAX company made a short film called: *The Blue Planet*. This film was made in a space shuttle. It is shown on a huge, concave screen with sounds coming from all sides. The viewers feel as if they are, in fact, sitting in the shuttle. The most remarkable part of this film is that it allows us to see what the astronauts were seeing: our own planet. For the first time in human history, we are able to see the earth from a distance. As we look at our earth, we come to the realization that this beautiful blue ball, moving through the universe, is our own home. We can say: 'Look, that's where we live, that's where we work, that's where we have our family, that's our home. Isn't that a beautiful place to live!' As we look at that beautiful, majestic, blue planet as our home, we suddenly have a completely new understanding of the word 'our'. 'Our' means all people, from all the continents, of all colors, religions, races and ages. Seen from the space shuttle, the many differences among people that cause hatred, violence, war, oppression, starvation and mutual destruction seem completely ridiculous. From the distance of the space shuttle, it is crystal clear that we have the same home, that we belong together and that together we have to care for our beautiful blue planet so that we will be able to live there, not just now, but for the long, long future. Our space-age has made it possible for us to grow into a new consciousness of the basic unity of all people on the earth and the common responsibility of all people to care for each other and, together, to care for their home. Seeing our blue planet from a distance, we can say in a whole new way: 'We are indeed brothers and sisters as Jesus told us long ago. We all are born as fragile beings, we all die as fragile beings. We all need each other and our beautifully-made home to live well and to die well.'

The distant view of our home may make it possible for us to live and die with a new and deeper knowledge of being children of one God, brothers and sisters of each other and to truly care.

6

You Are the Parents of Generations to Come

Last year, during Holy Week, while having dinner with some friends in downtown Toronto, I received a phone call that Connie Ellis, my secretary and close friend for the past six years, had suddenly become ill and been brought to the hospital. Until late that afternoon, she had worked hard trying to finish a text that I needed to take with me to Europe after Easter. She had come home very tired and suddenly had felt disoriented and anxious. Happily, she was still able to call her daughter-in-law, Carmen. When Carmen heard Connie's slurred and barely understandable speech, she became very worried and hurried to see her at home.

The next day, tests showed that Connie had suffered a stroke, caused by a large brain tumor. On Good Friday, she underwent extensive surgery.

Although the surgery was 'successful,' it left her paralyzed on her left side, unable to walk by herself and in constant danger of falling. After extensive radiation therapy, doctors told her that the cancer was in remission. But she remained very fragile without much prospect that things would ever be normal again.

In one day, a strong, healthy, active and very efficient woman became fully dependent on family and friends. It was very painful for me to see my close friend and co-worker suddenly lose her ability to do many things and help many people. But it was also very hopeful for me to see that this radical change did not affect her trusting and loving disposition. Often she said to me: 'I feel deep inner peace. I am sure God will perform a miracle for me, but, if not, I am ready to die. I have had a very beautiful life.'

For years, Connie has been known for her great vitality, her competence and her ability to accomplish a lot in a very short time. For me, she had become my right as well as my left hand. She knew all the people who came to the office, phoned in or wrote and had developed a warm relationship with many of them. The help, support and advice she gave to countless people during the six years we worked together had made her a friend of many. Her ministry had become as important as my own. Then, in an instant, it was all over. She who had always been eager to help others now needed others to help her. This radical turn happened overnight.

As I reflect on this dramatic event in Connie's life and realize that she is, in fact, one of the many people who have similar experiences, I wonder what meaning to give it. We human beings cannot live without meaning. Whatever happens to us, we keep asking: 'Why is this happening to me . . . what does it mean?'

Much of the meaning of Connie's life came from her relationship to her two sons, John and Steve, and their families. Her close friendship with Steve's wife, Carmen, and with her two grandchildren, Charles and Sarah, especially, gave her great joy and satisfaction. One of Connie's joys was to take Charles to his hockey game, and encourage him on the side lines. I could be critical about anyone in her presence, but not about 'Carm and the kids.' They were simply beyond criticism! Much meaning also came from her work in the office. To the last minute of her working life, Connie enjoyed immensely what she was doing and did it with a never-abating dedication. I remember how happy she was that she had been able to transcribe all the interviews I had made with the five trapeze artists in the circus. She fervently supported me in my 'crazy' idea to write a book about them and wanted to be sure that I had all the necessary texts before returning to Germany for more interviews. Our work together, in all its variety and hecticness, gave a lot of meaning to her life. But few people realized that she was already past seventy and getting very tired at times.

When, suddenly, everything changed, the question of meaning returned in full force. For a while, the emphasis was on getting better and doing many things again. 'Once I can drive my car again,' Connie would say, 'I won't be so dependent on John, Steve, Carm and the kids any more and will be able to manage by myself again.' But she gradually came to see that this might never be possible. For the rest of her life, she might need others to help her.

Caring for Connie and for the many who can no longer expect to return to their work and who can no longer be of service to their family and friends, is searching together for new meaning. And this new meaning can no longer be drawn from activities to get things done. Somehow, it has to grow out of the 'passivities' of waiting.

Jesus' life was a life that moved from action to passion. For several years he was extremely active: preaching, teaching, and helping, always surrounded by large crowds and always moving from place to place. But in the Garden of Gethsemane, after his last supper with his disciples, he was handed over to those who resented him and his words. He was handed over to passion. From that moment, Jesus no longer took initiatives. He no longer did anything. Everything was done to him.

He was arrested, put in prison, ridiculed, tortured, condemned and crucified. All action was gone, all had become passion. The mystery of Jesus' life is that he fulfilled his vocation, not through action, but through passion, through becoming the subject of other people's actions. When he finally said 'It is fulfilled' (John 19:30), he meant not only, 'All I needed to do I have done', but also 'All that needed to be done to me has been done to me.' Jesus completed his mission on earth in passion, through being the passive subject of what others did to him.

What Jesus lived we also are called to live. Our lives, when lived in the spirit of Jesus, will find their fulfillment in passion. Jesus makes this very clear when he says to Peter: 'When you were young, you put on your belt and walked where you liked, but when you grow old, you will stretch out your hands and somebody else will put a belt round you and take you where you would rather not go' (John 21:18). We too, have to move from action to passion, from being in control to being dependent, from taking initiatives to having to wait, from living to dying.

Painful and nearly impossible as this move seems to be, it is the movement in which our true fruitfulness is hidden. Our years of action are the years of success and accomplishment. During these years we do things about which we can speak with pride. But much of this success and many of these accomplishments will soon lie behind us. Maybe we can still point to them in the form of trophies, medals or artistic products. But what is there beyond our success and productivity? It is our fruitfulness and that fruitfulness comes through passion. Just as the ground can only bear fruit as it is broken by the plough, so too, our own lives can only be fruitful when they have been opened through passion, that is, suffering. Suffering is precisely 'undergoing' action by others over whom we have no control. Dying is always suffering because dying always puts us in the place where others do to us whatever they decide to do — good or bad.

It is not easy to trust that it is through passion that our lives will bear fruit because, for the most part, we ourselves experience dependency as uselessness and being a burden. We often feel discomfort, fatigue, confusion, disorientation and pain, and it is hard to see any fruit coming from such vulnerability. What we see is a body and a mind broken to pieces by the plow that others hold in their hands!

It requires a tremendous leap of faith to believe that our lives come to fulfillment in passion. Everything that we, ourselves, see or feel, as well as everything that our society suggests to us through the values and ideas it holds up to us, points in the opposite direction. Success, not fruitfulness, is what counts and certainly not when it comes through passion. But passion is God's way, shown to us through the cross of Jesus. It's the way we want to avoid at all costs, but it is the way to salvation. This explains why it is so important to care for the dying. Because to care for the dying is to help the dying make that hard move from action to passion, from success to fruitfulness, from wondering how much they can still accomplish to making their very lives a gift for others. Caring for the dying means helping the dying discover that, in their increasing weakness, God's strength becomes visible. The well-known words of the Apostle Paul, 'God chose those who by human standards are weak to shame the strong' (1 Cor. 1:27), take on a new meaning here because the weak are not only the poor, the handicapped and the mentally ill, but also the dying. And all of us will be dying one day. We have to trust that it is also in this weakness that God shames the strong and reveals true human fruitfulness. That's the mystery of the cross. On the cross Jesus' life became infinitely fruitful. There, the greatest weakness and the greatest strength met. It is in this mystery that we can participate through our death. To help each other die well is to help each other claim our fruitfulness in our weakness. Thus, our dying enables us to embrace our cross with the trust that new life will emerge.

Much of this becomes very concrete when we are with people who have to come to terms with their approaching death.

After her brain surgery Connie always expressed a double desire: the desire for 'a miracle' — as she called it — to be completely cured and to be able to resume a normal life and the desire to die peacefully without causing too much grief to her children and grandchildren. As it became clear that a full cure was unlikely to occur, she began to think and speak more about her death and how to prepare herself and her family for it.

I remember vividly how, one day, she said to me: 'I am not afraid to die. I feel safe in God's love. I know that you and many others pray for me every day and that nothing bad can happen to me, but . . . I worry about the kids.' As she said this she began to cry. I knew how close she felt to her grand-children, Charles and Sarah, and how much their lives, their happiness and their future concerned her. I asked her: 'What are you thinking?' She said: 'I don't want the kids to suffer because of me. I don't want them to become sad and sorrowful as they see me dying. They always knew me as the strong grandmother they could count on. They don't know me as a paralyzed woman whose hair is falling out because of radiation therapy. I worry when I look into their faces and see them so anxious and sad. I want them to be happy children, now, and after I am gone.' Connie didn't think about herself. She thought first of others. She wanted to be sure that I would find a good person to take over her work in the office. She wanted to be sure that her illness would not interrupt the life of her children and their families. But most of all she wanted her grandchildren, Sarah and Charles, to be happy people. She worried that her sickness and death would prevent that.

As I saw Connie's pain, I saw more than ever what a beautiful, generous, caring person she is. She cares deeply for all the people who are part of her life. *Their* well-being is more important for her than her own. *Their* work, *their* pleasures and *their* dreams concern her more than her own. In this society in which most people are so self-centred, Connie is a true ray of light.

Still, I wanted Connie to move beyond her worries and trust that her love for her family and friends would be fruitful. I wanted her to believe that what was important was not only what she did or still could do for others, but also — and ever more so — what she lives in her illness and how she lives it. I wanted her to come to see that, in her growing dependency, she is giving more to her grandchildren than during the times when she could drive them around in her car and bring them to school, to shops and to sports fields. I wanted her to discover that the times when she needs them are as important as the times when they need her. The fact is that in her illness she has become their real teacher. She speaks to them about her gratitude for life, her trust in God and her hope in a life beyond death. She shows them real thankfulness for all the little things they do for her. She doesn't keep her tears or fears hidden from them when they suddenly well up, but she always returns to a smile.

Most of her own goodness and love she can't see herself. But I, and the many people who visit her can see it. She, who lived such a long and very productive life now, in her growing weakness, gives what she couldn't give in her strength: a glimpse of the truth that love is stronger than death. Her grandchildren will reap the full fruits of that truth.

In our dying, we become parents of the generations to come. How true this is of many holy people! Through their weakness, they gave us a view of God's grace. They are still close to us: St Francis of Assisi, Martin Luther, John Henry Newman, Therese de Lisieux, Mahatma Gandhi, Thomas Merton, John XXIII, Dag Hammarskjold, Dorothy Day and many others who belonged to our own little circle of family and friends. Our thoughts and feelings, our words and writings, our dreams and visions are not just our own: they belong also to the many men and women who have died already and are now living within us. Their lives and deaths are still bearing fruit in our lives. Their joy, hope, courage, confidence and trust didn't die with them but continue to blossom in our hearts and the hearts of the many who are connected with us in love. Indeed they keep sending the Spirit of

Jesus to us and give us the strength to be faithful in the journey we have begun.

We, too, must see to it that our deaths become fruitful in the lives of those who will live after us. Without care, however, it is difficult, if not impossible, to let our lives bear fruit in the generations to come. Devoid of care, our society makes us believe that we are what we have, what we do, or what people think about us. With such a belief, our death is, indeed, the end because when we die, all property, success and popularity vanish. Without care for each other we forget who we truly are — children of God and each other's brothers and sisters — and so cannot become parents of the generations to come. But as a community of care, we can remind each other that we will bear fruit far beyond the few years we have to live. As a community of care, we trust that those who live long after we have lived, will still receive the fruits of the seeds we have sown in our weakness and find new strength in them. As a community of care, we can send the Spirit of Jesus to each other. Thus, we become the fruit-bearing people of God that embraces past, present and future and so is a light in the darkness.

I would like to conclude this final chapter by telling the story of our meals in the Daybreak community because they show something about fruitfulness born in weakness.

The meals in the Daybreak houses are the high

points of our daily life. They are like small celebrations. The food is eaten slowly because many of us cannot eat by ourselves and need to be fed. The conversations around the table are very simple because many of us cannot speak, and those who can don't use many words. The prayers are always for others; each one mentioned by name because, for people with mental handicaps, what really counts are other people. Often there are candles and flowers, and on special occasions there are banners and balloons.

Whenever I am part of such a meal, I become acutely aware that the gifts of the Spirit of Jesus are given to us in weakness. While many of us experience much physical or emotional pain, while quite a few cannot make a move without assistance and while some have few ways to communicate their needs and desires, still, the spiritual gifts of peace, joy, gentleness, forgiveness, hope and trust are very much present there. It seems that our shared vulnerability is the favorite climate for Jesus to show us his love, for it is certainly not we who have created these gifts of love. We wouldn't even know how to go about it! Many of us are too pre-occupied with just surviving or helping others to survive. And, as in all families and communities, there are tensions and conflicts too. Still, it seems that around this table of poverty, Jesus becomes powerfully present, generously sending his spirit.

During the time of prayer at the end of each meal, it becomes clear that these Daybreak meals have the quality of a memorial. We not only lift up our own life to God in gratitude, but also the lives of those of whose weakness we are aware and especially, the lives of those who are dying or have died. Thus we make them all part of our 'fellowship of weakness.'

And aren't these memorial meals also ways in which we care for each other and prepare each other to accept our final vulnerability? There is little chance that anyone will ever talk about our evening dinners as 'last suppers,' but still we want to say to each other: 'When I am no longer here, keep remembering me whenever you come together to eat, drink and celebrate, and I in return will send you the Spirit of Jesus who will deepen and strengthen the bonds of love that bind you together.' And so every meal in which we remember Jesus and those who died in him also prepares us for our own death. And so, we not only feed ourselves but also nurture each other and thereby become, each day, a little more the community of care to which we always will belong.

The Choice to Care Well

To care well for the dying, we must trust deeply that they are loved as much as we are, and we must make that love visible by our presence; we must also trust that their dying and deaths deepen their solidarity with the human family and we must guide them in becoming part of the communion of saints; finally we must trust that their deaths, just as ours, will make their lives fruitful for generations to come, and we must encourage them to let go of their fears, and hope beyond the boundaries of death.

Caring well, just as dying well, asks for a choice. Although we all carry within us the gift to care, this gift can only become visible when we choose it.

We are constantly tempted to think that we have nothing or little to offer to our fellow human beings.

Their despair frightens us. It often seems better not to come close than to come close without being able to change anything. This is especially true in the presence of people who face death. But in running away from the dying we bury our precious gift of care.

Still, whenever we claim our gift of care and choose to embrace not only our own, but also other people's mortality, we can become a true source of healing and hope. When we have the courage to let go of our need to cure, our care can truly heal in ways far beyond our own dreams and expectations. With our gift of care we can gently lead our dying brothers and sisters always deeper into the heart of God and God's universe.

CONCLUSION

The Grace of the Resurrection

Nearly three weeks have passed since I started to write this little book on dying well, and caring well. Although I have, for the most part, kept to my little hermitage on the third floor of Franz and Reny's house, I have been with many people, some in person, most in thought. I have been with Maurice in Daybreak, Rick in Oakland, Marina in Rotterdam and Connie in Richmond Hill. I have 'visited' countless people in Europe, Asia, Africa and Latin America who are dying as the result of war, starvation and oppression, and I have tried to embrace with my heart those who have lived and died but continue to inform and inspire me with their actions and words.

During all these extensive mental travels, I have tried to claim for myself as well as for others, that we are children of God, sisters and brothers of each other and parents of future generations. I have attempted to explore the ways in which this spiritual identity offers us not only a vision of how to die well ourselves, but also a vision of how to care well for others who are dying. The words: intimacy, solidarity and fruitfulness have emerged as parts of this vision.

As I sit now behind my desk writing this conclusion, I realize a question may have come to those reading these words: 'What of the Resurrection?' It surprises me that so far I have neither written about the Resurrection nor felt any need to do so. It simply didn't seem an urgent question as I was writing. But the fact that the Resurrection didn't present itself with great urgency does not mean that it isn't important. To the contrary, the Resurrection is more important than any of the things of which I have written so far because the Resurrection is the foundation of my faith. To write about dying and death without mentioning the Resurrection is like writing about sailing without ever mentioning the wind! The Resurrection of Jesus and the hope of our resurrection have made it possible for me to write about dying and death in the way I have. With Paul the apostle, I dare to say: '...If Christ is proclaimed as raised from the dead, how can some of you be saying that there is no resurrection of the dead? For, if the dead are not raised, neither is Christ, and if Christ has not been raised, your faith is pointless and you have not, after all, been released from your sins. In addition, those who have fallen asleep in Christ are utterly lost. If our hope in Christ has been for this life only, we are of all people the most pitiable' (1 Cor. 15:12–18).

It hardly seems possible to have a stronger opinion about the Resurrection than Paul expresses in these words, and I want to make Paul's words my own. Still, I have not yet written about the Resurrection of Jesus and our own. I think that my hesitation in writing about the Resurrection is connected with my conviction that the Resurrection of Jesus is a very hidden event. Jesus didn't rise from the dead to prove to those who had crucified him that they had made a mistake, or confound his opponents. Nor did he rise to impress the rulers of his time or to force anyone to believe. Jesus's Resurrection was the full affirmation of his Father's love. Therefore, he showed himself only to those who knew about this love. He made himself known as the risen Lord, only to a handful of his close friends. There is probably no event in human history that has had such importance, while remaining, at the same time, so unspectacular. The world didn't notice it; only those few to whom Jesus had chosen to show himself, and whom he wanted to send out to announce God's love to the world, just as he had done.

The hiddenness of Jesus' Resurrection is important to me. Although the Resurrection of Jesus is the cornerstone of my faith, it is not an argument or a way to prove something nor even a way to reassure people. Saying to dying people: 'Don't be afraid. After your death you will be resurrected as Jesus was, meet all your friends again and be forever happy in the presence of God,' somehow doesn't take death seriously enough and suggests that, after death everything will be basically the same — except for our troubles. Nor does it take seriously Jesus himself, who didn't live through his own death as if it were little else than a necessary passage to a better life. And, finally, it doesn't take seriously the dying who, like we, know nothing about what is beyond this time- and place-bound existence.

The Resurrection is not a solution for our problems about dying and death. It's not the happy ending to our life's struggle, nor is it the big surprise that God has kept in store for us. No, the Resurrection is the expression of God's faithfulness to Jesus and to all God's children. Through the Resurrection, God is saying to Jesus, 'You are, indeed, my Beloved Son, and my love is everlasting', and to us: 'You, indeed, are my Beloved children and my love is everlasting.' The Resurrection is God's way of revealing to us that nothing that belongs to God will ever go to waste. What belongs to God will never get lost, not even our mortal bodies! The Resurrection, therefore, doesn't answer any of our curious questions about life after death, such as, 'How will it be? How will it look?' It does, however, reveal to us that, indeed, love is stronger than death. After that revelation we have to remain silent and leave the 'whys, wheres, hows and whens' behind ... and simply trust.

On the occasion of his ninetieth birthday, my father gave an interview to a Dutch radio station. After the reporter had asked him many questions about his life and work and even more about the current Dutch tax system – since that was my father's professional interest – he finally wanted to know what he thought would happen to him after his death.

I was obviously quite curious about what my father's answer would be to this last question. Sometimes it seems easier to get such an intimate answer sitting together in front of the radio than sitting across from each other at the dinner table! My father and I were both listening to the program that was broadcast a week after it was made. I heard my father say to the reporter: 'Well, I have very little to say about it. I don't really believe that I will see my wife or friends again as we see each other now. I don't have any concrete expectations. Yes, there is something else, but when there is no time and space any more, any word about that 'something else' wouldn't make much sense. I am not afraid to die. I don't desire to become one hundred years old. I just want to live my life now as good as I can and . . . when I die. Well, then we will see!'

Maybe my Father's belief as well as his unbelief, is best summarized in these last words: 'Well . . . we will see.' His scepticism and his faith touch each other in these words. 'Well . . . we will see' can mean 'Well . . . it's all up in the air,' but also 'Well, we finally will see what we always wanted to see!' We will see God, we will see one another. That's what Jesus is clear about when he says: 'Do not let your hearts be troubled. You trust in God, trust also in me. In my Father's house there are many places to live in; . . . I am going now to prepare a place for you and after I have gone and prepared you a place, I shall return to take you to myself, so that you may be with me where I am' (John 14: 1–4). And when Jesus appears to Mary of Magdala near the empty tomb, he sends her out with the words 'Go and find my brothers and tell them: I am ascending to my Father and your Father, to my God and your God' (John 20: 17).

The risen Jesus, eating and drinking with his friends, shows that God's love for us, our love for each other and our love for those who lived before and after us is not just a transitory experience, but an eternal reality transcending all time and space. And the risen Jesus, showing his pierced hands, feet and side to his friends also reveals that all we have lived in our body during our years on earth, our joyful as well as painful experiences, will not simply fall away from us as a useless cloak but will mark our unique way of being with God and each other as we make the passage of death.

'Well ... we will see'; these words will probably always have a double meaning. As the father of the epileptic boy, who asked Jesus to heal his child, we will always have to say: 'I believe. Help my unbelief' (Mark 9:24). Still, when we keep our eyes fixed on the risen Lord, we may find not only that love is stronger than death, but also that our faith is stronger than our scepticism.

EPILOGUE

Death: A Loss and A Gift

Yesterday afternoon, just as I was finishing the conclusion of this book, Jean Vanier called me from Trosly, France. In a very gentle way he said: 'Henri, Père Thomas died this morning.' Père Thomas Philippe, a French Dominican priest, was the spiritual father of Jean and the co-founder of L'Arche. He was a man aflame with love of Jesus, his Mother Mary and all the 'little' people in this world. This Pere Thomas, who inspired and encouraged his student and friend, Jean Vanier, to leave his teaching position in Toronto and start a life with handicapped people ... this holy and humble Dominican priest is now dead.

Listening to Jean's voice, I heard the voice of a man who had lost his mentor and has now to continue alone. I said: 'What a loss for you!' He replied, 'Yes a great loss for me and for L'Arche ... but also a great gift.' Père Thomas's death is indeed a loss and a gift. A loss, because so many found new hope just by thinking about him. I am one of them. During the most difficult period of my life, when I experienced great anguish and despair, he was there. Many times he pulled my head to his chest and prayed for me without words but with a spirit-filled silence that dispelled my demons of despair and made me rise up from his embrace with new vitality. Countless people were willing to wait for hours in the vestibule of his little room to be with him. People in despair, people with great mental suffering, people agonizing about the choices they had to make, people not knowing how to pray, people who couldn't believe in God, people with broken relationships and — during recent years — many people living with AIDS looking for someone to help them to die well. We all have lost our good shepherd, our 'crook and staff' in this valley of darkness and wonder how to keep going without him.

But, as Jean said, his death is a gift too. Now his life can bear full fruit. Père Thomas suffered immensely. He suffered from the Church he loved so much, especially when the Church closed the international community of students he had founded and no longer allowed him to continue his work as university chaplain. He suffered great loneliness when he came to the little village of Trosly in the north of France and began to minister there to a group of young men with mental disabilities. He suffered during the long hours he spent in front of the Blessed Sacrament in his little chapel, wondering what Jesus wanted of him, and — after having started L'Arche with Jean Vanier — he often suffered from feelings of being misunderstood and even rejected, especially when he saw developments taking place that were quite different from what he had expected. As he became older, he entered into an ever-deeper communion with Jesus on the cross and suffered with him great anguish and abandonment.

When, finally, Père Thomas could no longer be with so many people, he withdrew to the south of France where he lived for a few years in hiddenness. There he died a few days after Jean had visited him, and a few hours after his brother, Père Marie Dominique, had given him the Eucharist. That was yesterday, Thursday, February 4, 1993 at one in the morning. As Jean said, Père Thomas's death is not only a loss, but a gift too. It is the end of a great suffering and the beginning of a new fruitfulness in L'Arche, in the Church, in society and in the hearts of the many who mourn his death.

When I began to write this book, I wasn't thinking about Père Thomas, even though he has been my main spiritual guide since I came to L'Arche. Since his leaving Trosly, he had become so hidden that even I didn't always fully realize that he had not yet made the final passage. Now, it dawns on me how immensely lonely he must have been during those last years: alone as Jesus was alone on Golgotha, 'the place of the skull' (John 19: 17). But since Jean's telephone call, he is here with me. He is so much God's Beloved Child, brother of all those he cared for and father of so many, who will receive life from hearing about him, listening to his tapes, and reading his books. Seldom have I met a man who loved so deeply and intensely. He was truly on fire with love. So much did he love that he dared to say to me: 'When you can't sleep during the night, just think of me and you will be fine.' He had such confidence in the Spirit of Jesus blazing in him that he didn't say: 'Think of God' or 'Think of Jesus' or 'Think of the Spirit', but 'Think of me'! It was this burning love that made him heal so many and suffer so much. It was this love that penetrated every part of his being and made him into a living prayer; a prayer with eyes, hands and a mouth that could only see, touch and speak of God. It was this love that consumed him as it consumed Jesus and gave life as it was consumed. It was this love that could not and cannot die, but only grow and grow.

The death of Père Thomas is given to me today to end this book. Père Thomas was a great gift to Jean, to me and to many others. Now he is a gift to all people. Now he can send the Spirit of Jesus to everyone, and the Spirit can blow where and when it pleases.

Tomorrow, Saturday, February 6, I will leave

Freiburg to go to France. I had not thought of leaving so soon — I have only been here three weeks — but after Jean's call I want to be in Trosly where Père Thomas's body will be brought and buried. I no longer want to be by myself in my little apartment writing about dying well and caring well. I want to be with that great community of people, poor and rich, young and old, strong and weak, gathered around the body of the man who loved so much and has been loved so much. As I travel from Freiburg to Strassburg, from Strassburg to Paris, from Paris to Compiègne and from there to Trosly, I will think my thoughts and pray my prayers in communion with Moe, Rick, Marina, Connie and my father, about whom I wrote in this book, but I will feel especially close to Thomas Philippe, that beautiful man, in whom the Spirit of Jesus was so fully alive and active. And in that large crowd of people mourning and giving thanks while breaking bread together in his memory, I will know as never before, that God indeed is love.